shortwave, the challenges it faces in a rapidly evolving landscape, and the enduring relevance of this timeless ı

"Shortwave Radio Mastery: A Listener's Journey" is more than just a guide; it's an invitation to share in the wonder of a world where the airwaves are a gateway to adventure and understanding. Whether you are a curious newcomer or a dedicated aficionado, we hope this book ignites your passion for shortwave radio and guides you towards a lifetime of rewarding exploration.

So, fasten your seatbelt, put on your headphones, and get ready to set sail into the boundless sea of shortwave radio. Your listener's journey begins now. Enjoy the ride!

Happy listening,

SREEKUMAR V T

COPYRIGHT WARNING

SHORTWAVE RADIO MASTERY

A Listener's Journey

SREEKUMAR V T

PREFACE

Welcome to "Shortwave Radio Mastery: A Listener's Journey."
Within the pages of this book, we invite you to embark on an
extraordinary voyage into the world of shortwave radio, a
realm where the airwaves carry stories, sounds, and secrets from around the
globe. This journey is not just about mastering the technical aspects of radio
reception; it's about uncovering the magic, wonder, and boundless
possibilities that the shortwave spectrum holds.

Shortwave radio has an enduring allure that has captivated enthusiasts for
decades. Its mystique lies in the ability to connect with far-flung corners of
the world, to eavesdrop on foreign cultures, and to discover the unexpected.
It is a realm where you can listen to distant music, unravel clandestine
espionage transmissions, or simply enjoy the mellifluous accents of news
broadcasters from every continent.

In "Shortwave Radio Mastery," we aim to provide you with a
comprehensive and in-depth exploration of this captivating hobby. Whether
you are a novice seeking to learn the basics or a seasoned DXer looking to
enhance your skills, this book is designed to be your faithful companion on
this thrilling journey.

Each chapter will be a portal into a new aspect of shortwave radio. From
understanding the science behind propagation to mastering the intricacies of
antenna design, from decoding exotic broadcasts to joining the global
community of radio enthusiasts, our goal is to equip you with the
knowledge, tools, and inspiration to become a true master of the shortwave.

Moreover, this book delves into the rich history of shortwave radio, its
pivotal role in times of conflict and peace, and its significance in fostering
cultural exchange and diplomacy. We'll also explore the future of

CONTENTS

1. WAVES OF INTRIGUE:

The World of Shortwave Radio

In the vast ocean of electromagnetic waves, there exists a realm where ordinary radio signals cannot tread – the realm of shortwave radio. For many, the world of shortwave radio is a mysterious and captivating place, brimming with intrigue and wonder. It's a realm where the waves carry the whispers of distant lands, where global communication transcends boundaries, and where listeners become explorers of the airwaves. In this chapter, we embark on a journey to explore the intriguing world of shortwave radio, setting the stage for an adventure that will unravel the secrets and stories concealed in the ether.

The Shortwave Spectrum: A World of Wonders

The shortwave spectrum, also known as high-frequency (HF) radio, ranges from 3 to 30 MHz. Within this comparatively narrow band of frequencies, a universe of broadcasts and signals awaits discovery. Shortwave radio has the unique ability to propagate over great distances due to its interactions with the Earth's ionosphere. As a result, shortwave signals can skip along the atmosphere, allowing them to reach listeners on the other side of the planet. It's this extraordinary characteristic that forms the foundation of shortwave radio's global reach.

Atmospheric Propagation: The Magic of Skip

To truly appreciate the world of shortwave radio, it's essential to understand the underlying science of atmospheric propagation. At the heart of this concept lies the ionosphere, a region of the Earth's upper atmosphere where the sun's radiation ionizes the gases, creating layers with varying degrees of electron density. Shortwave signals are bounced off these layers, allowing them to "skip" over the horizon.

The phenomenon of skip, or "skywave" propagation, enables shortwave signals to travel over thousands of kilometers, defying the line-of-sight limitation that characterizes lower-frequency radio waves. Skip distances can vary depending on factors like solar activity, time of day, and the frequency of the signal. DXers (long-distance radio enthusiasts) often chase these elusive skips, seeking distant and exotic broadcasts.

A World of Voices and Cultures

Shortwave radio is a cultural melting pot. Tune in to the shortwave bands, and you'll encounter an extraordinary array of voices, languages, and music. It's a place where you can hear news from the heart of Africa, listen to live folk music in Eastern Europe, or catch an interview with an Australian author. The sheer diversity of programming is one of the hallmarks of shortwave radio. It's a direct channel to the world's cultures and stories.

International broadcasters, government stations, religious organizations, and independent producers all find a home on shortwave. Whether it's the BBC World Service, Voice of America, or Radio Japan, these broadcasters strive to reach audiences far beyond their borders. They offer a window into their respective nations and promote cross-cultural understanding.

For listeners, shortwave radio is a passport to a multicultural journey. You can explore the culinary traditions of India in the morning, delve into Middle Eastern politics in the afternoon, and unwind with Latin American music in the evening – all from the comfort of your listening post.

Spy Games and Number Stations

The intrigue of shortwave radio extends beyond cultural exchanges. This realm has played a pivotal role in international espionage and covert communications. During the Cold War, shortwave frequencies were used by intelligence agencies to transmit secret messages. One of the most enigmatic aspects of this clandestine world is the existence of number stations.

Number stations are shortwave stations that broadcast sequences of numbers, letters, or other coded messages, often in a robotic or synthetic voice. The purpose of these stations remains shrouded in secrecy, and they have led to a plethora of conspiracy theories. It's widely believed that number stations were used by intelligence agencies to communicate with spies in the field. To this day, some number stations continue to broadcast, adding an element of intrigue to the shortwave landscape.

Shortwave as a Lifeline: Emergencies and Disaster Communications

While shortwave radio offers a diverse array of broadcasts, it also serves as a vital lifeline during times of crisis. When natural disasters strike and conventional communication infrastructure fails, shortwave radio often remains the last reliable means of receiving and transmitting information. Emergency services, such as the Red Cross, use shortwave frequencies to coordinate relief efforts. Amateurs, known as ham radio operators, step in to provide critical communication when all else fails.

In these trying times, shortwave radio becomes a beacon of hope, connecting survivors with the outside world and facilitating the exchange of critical information.

Shortwave Radio Communities: A Shared Passion

The world of shortwave radio is not just about solitary listening. It's also a realm of vibrant communities. Enthusiasts, listeners, and DXers come together to share their experiences, discoveries, and knowledge. Clubs, online forums, and gatherings provide a platform for shortwave aficionados to connect with like-minded individuals.

These communities help newcomers learn the ropes, offering guidance on equipment, antenna setups, and decoding techniques. Experienced DXers share their wisdom, recount their adventures, and provide updates on rare or noteworthy broadcasts. The camaraderie and the sense of belonging to a worldwide network of listeners enrich the shortwave radio experience.

Listening Post Setup: Your Gateway to the World

To explore the world of shortwave radio, you need to establish a listening post, also known as a shack. The foundation of your shack includes a good-quality shortwave receiver and an appropriate antenna. A well-designed listening post is crucial for optimal reception. In this chapter, we'll explore the different types of receivers and antennas available, as well as the techniques for setting up your listening post for a fantastic listening experience.

Conclusion

The world of shortwave radio is a captivating and ever-evolving landscape. Its ability to traverse continents, languages, and cultures makes it a unique medium for those who seek to explore, learn, and connect with the world. In this chapter, we've barely scratched the surface of what shortwave radio has to offer. The journey has just begun, and as we delve deeper into "Shortwave Radio Mastery: A Listener's Journey," we'll unlock more of the secrets and stories concealed within the ether, helping you to become a true master of the shortwave. So, fasten your seatbelt, put on your headphones, and prepare for a remarkable expedition into the waves of intrigue. The listener's journey continues.

Continue reading in the subsequent chapters to further your understanding and mastery of the captivating world of shortwave radio.

2. SETTING UP YOUR LISTENING POST

Equipment and Antennas

In the world of shortwave radio, your listening post, often affectionately referred to as a "shack," is your gateway to the global airwaves. It's the heart of your shortwave radio journey, where signals from distant lands come to life, and where you become an active participant in the magic of the ether. This chapter explores the essential equipment and antennas required to set up your listening post, providing a foundation for an exhilarating and fulfilling shortwave radio experience.

Choosing the Right Shortwave Receiver

At the core of your listening post lies the shortwave receiver, the device that captures the radio signals and converts them into audible sound. Selecting the right receiver is crucial to ensure that you can effectively tune into the shortwave bands.

There are various types of shortwave receivers available, catering to the needs and preferences of different listeners. These include:

1. **Portable Receivers**: These are compact, handheld units that are highly portable and ideal for on-the-go listening. They're perfect for outdoor expeditions, DXpeditions, or simply relaxing in your garden.
2. **Desktop Receivers**: These larger units are designed for home use and often offer advanced features and superior performance.

They are suitable for dedicated listeners who want the best possible reception.

3. **Software-Defined Radios (SDRs)**: SDRs connect to your computer and use software to process and decode radio signals. They offer flexibility and are often favored by tech-savvy listeners who enjoy experimenting with different decoding modes.

When selecting a shortwave receiver, consider factors such as sensitivity, selectivity, frequency coverage, and available features. Some receivers are optimized for particular types of signals, like single-sideband (SSB) for amateur radio or DRM (Digital Radio Mondiale) for digital broadcasts. Research and read reviews to find a receiver that meets your specific listening goals.

Antennas: The Lifeline of Reception

Once you have your receiver, the next crucial element of your listening post is the antenna. The antenna is the lifeline of reception, and the right choice can significantly enhance your listening experience.

A few common types of antennas suitable for shortwave radio listening include:

1. **Long Wire Antennas**: A long wire antenna is a simple and cost-effective solution. It consists of a length of wire, often stretched between two points, connected to your receiver. The longer the wire, the better the reception. This type of antenna is ideal for beginners and can be extended horizontally or vertically.

2. **Dipole Antennas**: A dipole antenna consists of two lengths of wire, each connected to one side of your receiver. It's often suspended horizontally between two supports. Dipole antennas are excellent for receiving signals in specific directions and are relatively easy to install.

3. **Loop Antennas**: Loop antennas are designed for compact spaces. They are less affected by interference and can be rotated

to optimize signal reception from different directions. Loop antennas are a good choice for urban environments.

4. **Beam Antennas**: Beam antennas are high-gain directional antennas that allow for precise tuning into specific signals. They are more complex to set up and often require a rotor for precise positioning.

The choice of antenna depends on your location, available space, and listening preferences. If you have the space, a long wire antenna can be an excellent starting point. However, urban listeners with limited space might find loop antennas more practical. Experimentation is key, as fine-tuning your antenna setup often leads to improved reception.

Accessories and Peripherals

In addition to your receiver and antenna, there are various accessories and peripherals that can enhance your listening experience. Some of these include:

1. **External Speakers**: While most shortwave radios come with built-in speakers, connecting an external speaker can improve audio quality and make your listening experience more enjoyable.
2. **Headphones**: A good pair of headphones is essential for private listening and helps you pick up faint signals in noisy environments.
3. **Antenna Tuners**: Antenna tuners can help match the impedance of your antenna system to your receiver, optimizing signal reception.
4. **Baluns and Ununs**: These devices are used to transform impedance and improve antenna efficiency.
5. **Coaxial Cable**: High-quality coaxial cable is essential for connecting your antenna to your receiver and minimizing signal loss.
6. **Lightning Protection**: It's crucial to protect your equipment from lightning strikes by using lightning arrestors and grounding systems.

Setting Up Your Listening Post

With your equipment in hand, it's time to set up your listening post. Here are the key steps to consider:

1. **Choose the Right Location**: Select a location for your listening post that minimizes interference from household electronics and power lines. An outdoor location, like a garden or rooftop, can offer better reception due to reduced interference.
2. **Install the Antenna**: Set up your chosen antenna, ensuring it's as far away as possible from sources of electromagnetic interference. Use non-conductive supports and keep safety in mind, especially when installing outdoor antennas.
3. **Connect the Receiver**: Attach your receiver to the antenna using the appropriate coaxial cable. Ensure that all connections are secure to prevent signal loss.
4. **Grounding and Lightning Protection**: If you're using an outdoor antenna, implement grounding and lightning protection to safeguard your equipment from electrical surges.
5. **Tuning and Calibration**: Turn on your receiver, tune to a shortwave frequency, and adjust the antenna for optimal signal strength. You may need to fine-tune your antenna and receiver settings to achieve the best reception.
6. **External Equipment**: If you're using external speakers, headphones, or other peripherals, connect them to your receiver.
7. **Recording and Logging**: Consider using a notebook or digital log to record interesting stations, signal details, and any noteworthy broadcasts.
8. **Experimentation**: Don't be afraid to experiment with your setup. Moving your antenna, adjusting its length, or trying different types of antennas can yield significant improvements in reception.

Antenna Tuning and Matching

One critical aspect of setting up your listening post is antenna tuning and matching. These processes are essential for optimizing your antenna's performance and ensuring that it receives signals most effectively.

Antenna tuning involves adjusting the physical length or configuration of your antenna to resonate at specific frequencies. Matching refers to adjusting the impedance of your antenna system to match the input impedance of your receiver.

An antenna tuner (or transmatch) can be a valuable tool in this process, allowing you to fine-tune your antenna to achieve a better match and resonance. Some receivers also have built-in antenna tuners, simplifying this task.

Interference and Noise Reduction

Interference and noise can be significant challenges in shortwave radio listening, particularly in urban environments. Sources of interference can include power lines, household appliances, and electronic devices. To minimize interference:

1. **Select the Best Location**: Choose a location as far away from sources of interference as possible.
2. **Use Loop or Magnetic Antennas**: Loop antennas are less susceptible to interference, making them a good choice for urban listeners.
3. **Ferrite Cores**: Attach ferrite cores to your coaxial cable to reduce common-mode interference.
4. **Noise Blankers**: Some receivers have noise blanker functions that can help eliminate impulse noise.
5. **Noise Reduction Software**: Consider using digital signal processing (DSP) software to reduce noise in the audio output of your receiver.

Maintenance and Care

Proper maintenance of your listening post equipment is essential to ensure optimal performance and longevity. Here are some maintenance tips:

1. **Cleaning**: Keep your equipment clean and free of dust or debris that may affect its performance.
2. **Cable Inspection**: Regularly inspect coaxial cables for wear or damage and replace them if necessary.

3. **Grounding Inspection**: Check your grounding and lightning protection systems for any signs of corrosion or damage.
4. **Antenna Check**: Inspect your antenna connections and supports to ensure they remain secure.
5. **Antenna Adjustment**: Periodically fine-tune your antenna and check for signs of sagging or damage.
6. **Receiver Calibration**: Occasionally, recalibrate your receiver if you notice a drop in performance.

Conclusion

Setting up your listening post is a vital step on your journey of shortwave radio mastery. The combination of the right equipment, a well-chosen antenna, and careful tuning will open the door to a world of diverse broadcasts, cultural exchanges, and long-distance connections.

Remember that your listening post is not static. As you gain experience, you may decide to experiment with different antennas, receivers, and accessories. The key is to embrace the ever-evolving nature of shortwave radio and continue to fine-tune your setup to maximize your listening experience.

In the chapters that follow in "Shortwave Radio Mastery: A Listener's Journey," we'll delve further into the world of shortwave radio, exploring techniques for effective listening, unraveling the intricacies of decoding various signals, and embarking on global adventures through the airwaves. Your journey has just begun, and there's a world of radio signals waiting to be discovered. Happy listening!

Continue reading in the subsequent chapters to further your understanding of shortwave radio and embark on an exciting listener's journey.

3.TUNING IN

Understanding Shortwave Bands

I n the realm of shortwave radio, understanding the intricacies of the shortwave bands is akin to having a map that guides you through an uncharted territory. These bands are the frequencies on which the magic of shortwave communication happens, where voices, music, news, and data traverse the globe, connecting distant lands and cultures. To embark on your journey into the world of shortwave radio, you must first grasp the composition of these bands, the frequencies they encompass, and the treasures they hold. In this chapter, we will unravel the mysteries of the shortwave bands, providing you with the knowledge you need to become a proficient shortwave radio enthusiast.

The Shortwave Spectrum

The shortwave spectrum, often referred to as high-frequency (HF) radio, is a unique and magical portion of the radio frequency spectrum. It covers the frequency range from approximately 3 to 30 MHz. Unlike the lower-frequency AM (amplitude modulation) or FM (frequency modulation) bands, which are primarily used for local and regional broadcasts, the shortwave spectrum has the extraordinary ability to propagate signals across continents and oceans.

This propagation phenomenon is a result of the interaction between shortwave radio signals and the Earth's ionosphere. As shortwave signals encounter the ionosphere, they may refract or "skip" off it, allowing them to travel great distances. This characteristic is the key to shortwave's global reach and makes it an exciting playground for radio enthusiasts.

Exploring the Shortwave Bands

The shortwave spectrum is divided into several distinct bands, each with its unique characteristics and purposes. Here, we will explore the main shortwave bands, their frequency ranges, and the types of broadcasts commonly found within them:

1. **Medium-Frequency (MF) Band**: While not technically in the shortwave spectrum, the MF band, encompassing frequencies from 530 to 1700 kHz, often serves as a bridge to the shortwave bands. Many international broadcasters operate in both the MF and shortwave bands to reach a broader audience.
2. **Low-Frequency (LF) Band**: Frequencies in the LF band, ranging from 30 to 300 kHz, are often used for maritime and navigation purposes. While not typically associated with shortwave listening, these frequencies can carry important signals for navigational aids and maritime communication.
3. **Very Low Frequency (VLF) Band**: Frequencies from 3 to 30 kHz are considered part of the VLF band. VLF signals are primarily used for military and scientific applications, including submarine communication and time signal broadcasts. They are not a common focus of shortwave radio enthusiasts.
4. **30-Meter Band**: The 30-meter band spans from 10.100 to 10.150 MHz. It is often used by amateur radio operators (hams) for digital modes and CW (continuous wave) communication.
5. **20-Meter Band**: Frequencies in the 20-meter band range from 14.000 to 14.350 MHz. This band is a favorite among amateur radio operators, and it hosts numerous DX (long-distance) contacts and contests.
6. **17-Meter Band**: Covering frequencies from 18.068 to 18.168 MHz, the 17-meter band is another popular choice for amateur radio enthusiasts, especially for DXing and casual conversation.
7. **15-Meter Band**: The 15-meter band, spanning from 21.000 to 21.450 MHz, is known for its excellent propagation conditions during periods of high solar activity. It's a preferred band for amateur radio operators chasing DX contacts.

8. **12-Meter Band**: Frequencies in the 12-meter band range from 24.890 to 24.990 MHz. While it's less commonly used than some other bands, it still offers opportunities for amateur radio communication.

9. **10-Meter Band**: The 10-meter band, extending from 28.000 to 29.700 MHz, is well-known for its strong sporadic-E propagation during certain times of the year. It's a favorite for amateur radio operators and even accommodates FM voice communication.

10. **CB Band**: Although not a traditional shortwave band, the Citizens Band (CB) frequencies from 26.965 to 27.405 MHz are popular for local communication and are used by CB radio enthusiasts.

11. **International Broadcast Bands**: These are the bands where most international broadcasters transmit their signals. They are often referred to by their approximate meter bands. For example, the 31-meter band covers frequencies from about 9.400 to 9.900 MHz. The 49-meter band spans from approximately 5.900 to 6.200 MHz.

12. **Amateur Bands**: These bands are allocated for use by amateur radio operators and offer a wide range of frequencies for various modes of communication. The most popular shortwave amateur bands include the 40-meter, 20-meter, and 15-meter bands, among others.

Shortwave Broadcast Bands

The shortwave broadcast bands are the treasure troves of international radio communication. These bands are home to a wide range of programming, from news and cultural content to music and educational broadcasts. Let's explore these broadcast bands in more detail:

- **60-Meter Band (4.750 - 5.060 MHz)**: While not as common for international broadcasting, this band is sometimes used by tropical broadcasting stations, especially for communication within the Americas.

- **49-Meter Band (5.900 - 6.200 MHz)**: The 49-meter band is often a prime spot for international broadcasters. It is known for its nighttime propagation, making it an excellent choice for evening listening.
- **41-Meter Band (7.100 - 7.300 MHz)**: Frequencies in the 41-meter band are used by many international broadcasters, particularly for broadcasts directed to Asia.
- **31-Meter Band (9.400 - 9.900 MHz)**: The 31-meter band is one of the busiest and most popular shortwave bands for international broadcasting. It provides good daytime and evening reception for a variety of programs.
- **25-Meter Band (11.600 - 12.100 MHz)**: The 25-meter band is known for its clear reception conditions and is home to several international broadcasters targeting different regions.
- **22-Meter Band (13.570 - 13.870 MHz)**: Frequencies in the 22-meter band are often used for transmissions in languages spoken in regions such as South Asia and the Middle East.
- **19-Meter Band (15.100 - 15.900 MHz)**: This band is known for its exceptional reception quality and hosts a wide variety of international broadcasts throughout the day.
- **16-Meter Band (17.480 - 17.900 MHz)**: Frequencies in the 16-meter band are sometimes used for European and Middle Eastern broadcasts.

Amateur Radio Bands and DXing

In addition to international broadcasters, the shortwave bands are populated by amateur radio operators (hams). These operators use various bands to communicate, experiment with different modes, and engage in DXing (contacting stations in distant locations). The interaction between international broadcasters and amateur radio operators adds to the diversity of signals on the bands.

Amateur radio bands on shortwave, also known as the HF bands, include the 160-meter band, 80-meter band, 40-meter band, 30-meter band, 20-meter band, 17-meter band, 15-meter band, 12-meter band, and 10-meter band. Each of these bands offers unique propagation characteristics and opportunities for long-distance communication.

DXing, the art of chasing distant or rare signals, is a popular pastime among both amateur radio operators and shortwave radio enthusiasts. The thrill of making contact with stations in far-off countries or rare entities is a rewarding aspect of the hobby. International broadcasters also add to the DXing experience by transmitting their signals across the globe, providing listeners with the opportunity to log exotic stations.

Monitoring and Schedules

Shortwave radio is dynamic, with signals changing throughout the day and night due to factors like ionospheric conditions and solar activity. To make the most of your shortwave listening experience, it's essential to monitor the bands regularly. Familiarize yourself with the time schedules of international broadcasters, as different stations broadcast during specific time slots.

Monitoring international broadcasting schedules, often available online or in publications, allows you to plan your listening sessions and target specific stations and programs of interest. Additionally, certain bands exhibit better propagation characteristics at different times of the day, so understanding these patterns can improve your chances of hearing distant stations.

Conclusion

As you delve into the enchanting world of shortwave radio, understanding the shortwave bands and their characteristics is the key to unlocking the rich tapestry of global communication. The bands are like a vast spectrum of colors, each representing a unique opportunity to discover voices, music, news, and cultures from around the world.

In the following chapters of "Shortwave Radio Mastery: A Listener's Journey," we will delve deeper into the practical aspects of shortwave listening. From decoding various types of broadcasts to optimizing your listening experience, your journey through the shortwave bands is just beginning. So, tune in, explore, and prepare to be amazed by the wonders that shortwave radio has to offer.

Continue reading to further your understanding and mastery of shortwave radio as we explore the practical aspects of tuning in to fascinating broadcasts from across the globe.

4. THE LANGUAGE OF RADIO

Decoding Broadcast Schedules

T he world of shortwave radio is a realm of frequencies, signals, and broadcasts that stretch across continents, offering a fascinating and diverse tapestry of voices, music, news, and cultures. At the heart of this vast and magical landscape are the shortwave bands, each a unique channel for global communication. To embark on a journey of shortwave radio mastery, it is essential to comprehend the intricate web of frequencies and their characteristics that define the shortwave bands. In this chapter, we will demystify the shortwave bands, helping you gain the knowledge required to become a skilled shortwave radio enthusiast.

The Shortwave Spectrum: An Overview

Shortwave radio, also known as high-frequency (HF) radio, encompasses a range of frequencies that extend from about 3 to 30 megahertz (MHz). Unlike traditional AM or FM radio, which are typically limited to local and regional communication, shortwave radio has the remarkable ability to propagate signals over long distances. This remarkable reach is made possible by the interaction of shortwave signals with the Earth's ionosphere, which enables them to "skip" off the ionized layers, traveling far beyond the horizon.

The shortwave spectrum can be divided into various bands, each with its unique properties, strengths, and propagation characteristics. These bands, while technically part of the HF range, play a central role in global shortwave communication.

Medium-Frequency (MF) and Low-Frequency (LF) Bands

While MF and LF are not technically part of the shortwave spectrum, they serve as an essential transition from the long-wave bands to the HF shortwave bands. The MF band encompasses frequencies from 530 to 1700 kilohertz (kHz) and is widely used for AM broadcasting. It serves as a bridge between regional AM broadcasts and the wider world of shortwave. The LF band, with frequencies ranging from 30 to 300 kHz, is primarily used for navigation and maritime communication and is not a primary focus for shortwave radio enthusiasts.

The Key Shortwave Bands

1. **30-Meter Band (10.100 - 10.150 MHz)**: This band is often used by amateur radio operators (hams) for digital modes and continuous wave (CW) communication.
2. **20-Meter Band (14.000 - 14.350 MHz)**: Frequencies in this band are a popular choice for amateur radio operators and are known for their strong DX (long-distance) contacts and contests.
3. **17-Meter Band (18.068 - 18.168 MHz)**: The 17-meter band is a favorite among amateur radio enthusiasts for both DXing and casual conversation.
4. **15-Meter Band (21.000 - 21.450 MHz)**: Frequencies in this band often exhibit excellent propagation conditions during periods of high solar activity, making it a preferred choice for DX contacts.
5. **12-Meter Band (24.890 - 24.990 MHz)**: While less frequently used than some other bands, the 12-meter band still offers opportunities for amateur radio communication.
6. **10-Meter Band (28.000 - 29.700 MHz)**: The 10-meter band is known for strong sporadic-E propagation during specific times of the year, making it a favorite for amateur radio operators and even accommodating FM voice communication.
7. **Citizens Band (CB) (26.965 - 27.405 MHz)**: While not traditionally considered a shortwave band, the CB frequencies are widely used for local communication by CB radio enthusiasts.

8. **International Broadcast Bands**: These are the primary bands where most international broadcasters transmit their signals. They are often referred to by their approximate meter bands. For instance, the 31-meter band covers frequencies from about 9.400 to 9.900 MHz, and the 49-meter band spans from approximately 5.900 to 6.200 MHz.

Shortwave Broadcast Bands

The shortwave broadcast bands are where the true magic of global communication unfolds. These bands are home to a wide variety of programming, from news and cultural content to music and educational broadcasts. Let's delve into the primary shortwave broadcast bands:

- **60-Meter Band (4.750 - 5.060 MHz)**: While less commonly used for international broadcasting, the 60-meter band is sometimes employed by tropical broadcasting stations, especially for communication within the Americas.
- **49-Meter Band (5.900 - 6.200 MHz)**: The 49-meter band is often a prime choice for international broadcasters, known for its nighttime propagation conditions, making it an excellent band for evening listening.
- **41-Meter Band (7.100 - 7.300 MHz)**: Frequencies in the 41-meter band are used by many international broadcasters, particularly for broadcasts aimed at Asian audiences.
- **31-Meter Band (9.400 - 9.900 MHz)**: The 31-meter band is one of the busiest and most popular shortwave bands for international broadcasting. It offers good daytime and evening reception for a wide variety of programs.
- **25-Meter Band (11.600 - 12.100 MHz)**: Frequencies in the 25-meter band are known for clear reception conditions and host several international broadcasters targeting different regions.
- **22-Meter Band (13.570 - 13.870 MHz)**: This band often carries broadcasts in languages spoken in South Asia and the Middle East.

- **19-Meter Band (15.100 - 15.900 MHz):** The 19-meter band is celebrated for its exceptional reception quality and hosts a diverse array of international broadcasts throughout the day.
- **16-Meter Band (17.480 - 17.900 MHz):** Frequencies in the 16-meter band are sometimes used for broadcasts directed toward Europe and the Middle East.

Amateur Radio Bands and DXing

In addition to international broadcasters, the shortwave bands are home to amateur radio operators, often referred to as hams. These enthusiasts use various bands for communication, experimentation with different modes, and engagement in DXing (making contacts with distant stations). The interaction between international broadcasters and amateur radio operators adds to the richness and diversity of signals on the shortwave bands.

Amateur radio bands on shortwave, known as the HF bands, include the 160-meter band, 80-meter band, 40-meter band, 30-meter band, 20-meter band, 17-meter band, 15-meter band, 12-meter band, and 10-meter band. Each of these bands offers unique propagation characteristics, making them suitable for different modes of communication and DXing.

DXing, the art of chasing distant or rare signals, is a rewarding aspect of the hobby that can be pursued by both amateur radio operators and shortwave radio enthusiasts. The thrill of making contact with stations in far-off countries or rare entities adds a sense of adventure to shortwave listening. International broadcasters contribute to the DXing experience by transmitting their signals worldwide, allowing listeners to log exotic stations and broaden their horizons.

Monitoring and Schedules

Shortwave radio is dynamic, with signals changing throughout the day and night due to factors like ionospheric conditions and solar activity. To make the most of your shortwave listening experience, it is essential to monitor the bands regularly. Familiarizing yourself with the time schedules of international broadcasters is a valuable practice, as different stations broadcast during specific time slots.

Monitoring international broadcasting schedules, which are often available online or in publications, enables you to plan your listening sessions and target specific stations and programs of interest. Additionally, different bands exhibit better propagation conditions at various times of the day, so understanding these patterns can improve your chances of hearing distant stations.

Conclusion

Understanding the shortwave bands and their characteristics is akin to having a compass that guides you through the vibrant and dynamic world of shortwave radio. The bands are the channels through which the globe communicates, each offering unique treasures, experiences, and connections. As you delve deeper into "Shortwave Radio Mastery: A Listener's Journey," you'll learn how to harness the potential of these bands to explore distant lands, cultures, and voices.

In the chapters that follow, we'll delve into the practical aspects of shortwave radio listening. From tuning in to various types of broadcasts to fine-tuning your equipment for optimal performance, your journey into the world of shortwave radio has only just begun. So, tune in, explore, and prepare to be amazed by the wonders that shortwave radio has to offer.

Continue reading to further your understanding and mastery of shortwave radio as we explore the practical aspects of tuning in to fascinating broadcasts from across the globe.

5. DISTANT SIGNALS

Receiving Stations from Afar

Shortwave radio listening is a remarkable journey through the airwaves, connecting you to voices, music, news, and cultures from around the world. One of the most captivating aspects of this hobby is the ability to receive distant signals, stations broadcasting from thousands of miles away. These stations often defy the limits of geography, bringing you closer to places and people you might never have the opportunity to experience in person. In this chapter, we'll explore the fascinating world of receiving stations from afar, delving into the techniques, equipment, and strategies that allow you to chase the most distant and exotic signals on the shortwave bands.

The Thrill of Distant Signals

One of the most exhilarating experiences in shortwave radio listening is hearing a station that is thousands of miles away, often on the other side of the planet. These distant signals offer a sense of adventure and a connection to the broader world, making you feel like a true global explorer. But how do these signals travel such vast distances and how can you harness their magic?

Propagation and the Ionosphere

The secret to receiving distant shortwave signals lies in the interaction between the radio waves and the Earth's ionosphere. The ionosphere is a layer of the Earth's atmosphere that contains charged particles, and it has a profound effect on radio wave propagation.

During the day, the ionosphere is typically divided into several layers, including the D, E, and F layers. At night, the D and E layers disappear, leaving only the F layer. These layers can reflect or refract radio waves, allowing them to "skip" off the ionosphere and travel great distances. The angle at which the waves interact with the ionosphere determines where they will land, allowing signals to bounce and travel over the horizon.

The condition of the ionosphere is influenced by various factors, including the time of day, the sunspot cycle, and solar activity. During periods of high solar activity, signals can propagate more effectively, leading to enhanced conditions for long-distance reception.

Equipment for Receiving Distant Signals

To chase distant signals effectively, it's essential to have the right equipment. While you can enjoy shortwave radio with a basic setup, enhancing your equipment can significantly improve your ability to receive distant stations. Here are some key components to consider:

1. **Shortwave Receiver**: Choose a high-quality shortwave receiver with excellent sensitivity and selectivity. Look for a receiver with multiple bandwidth options, which can help filter out interference and focus on weaker signals.
2. **Antenna**: The antenna plays a crucial role in signal reception. While a basic long wire antenna can suffice for local reception, a more sophisticated antenna system, like a directional antenna or a multi-element array, can enhance your ability to receive distant signals.
3. **Antenna Tuner**: An antenna tuner allows you to fine-tune your antenna's impedance to match your receiver's input, improving signal reception. It's particularly useful if you experiment with various antenna configurations.
4. **Preselector**: Some receivers come with built-in preselectors, which can filter out unwanted signals and interference before they reach the receiver's front end.
5. **Noise Reduction and Filters**: Noise reduction features and filters can help reduce interference, making distant signals clearer and more intelligible.

6. **Digital Signal Processing (DSP)**: Some modern receivers incorporate DSP technology to clean up and enhance incoming signals, particularly in challenging conditions.
7. **External Speaker or Headphones**: High-quality audio output can make a substantial difference in your ability to hear and understand distant signals.

Techniques for Receiving Distant Signals

Receiving distant signals is both an art and a science. It requires patience, skill, and a willingness to experiment. Here are some techniques to improve your chances of success:

1. **Select the Right Frequency**: Research the frequency bands and times when distant stations are most likely to be active. Use online resources, schedules, and frequency guides to plan your listening sessions.
2. **Understand Propagation**: Learn about the current ionospheric conditions, which are influenced by factors like solar activity, time of day, and season. Websites and tools that provide real-time ionospheric data can be invaluable for predicting propagation.
3. **Tune for Peak Reception**: As the ionosphere changes throughout the day, signals on different frequencies and bands will be more or less favorable for long-distance reception. Be ready to adjust your tuning as conditions evolve.
4. **Use Directional Antennas**: If you have access to directional antennas or antenna arrays, you can aim them at the target region to boost signal strength. Rotatable Yagi antennas are popular choices for this purpose.
5. **Antenna Placement**: Ensure your antenna is set up as far away as possible from sources of interference, such as power lines or electronic devices. Outdoor antennas are generally more effective for long-distance reception.
6. **Noise Reduction**: Use noise reduction features on your receiver and consider employing external noise reduction devices if you're dealing with significant interference.

7. **Experiment**: Don't be afraid to experiment with different antenna lengths, configurations, and positions. Small adjustments can make a significant difference in reception quality.
8. **Record and Review**: Record the signals you receive and listen to them later. You may catch details or station identifications that were not immediately apparent during the live broadcast.

Chasing DX: The Art of Distant Signal Reception

DXing, or distance listening, is a passionate pursuit among shortwave radio enthusiasts. DXers aim to receive signals from the farthest corners of the Earth, logging unique and rare stations. This hobby adds an element of competition and adventure, as DXers continuously seek to extend their reception boundaries.

To excel at DXing, consider these tips:

1. **Join DX Clubs**: DX clubs and online communities provide a platform to share your reception reports, learn from experienced DXers, and participate in contests and events.
2. **Keep a Logbook**: Maintain a logbook of your receptions, including details like the date, time, frequency, station name, and program content. This record is not only a testament to your DXing accomplishments but also a valuable resource for future listening.
3. **Seek Special Events**: Keep an eye out for special broadcasts and events, such as anniversary broadcasts or rare station activations, which can provide unique DX opportunities.
4. **Enhance Your Station**: Continually improve your equipment and antenna setup. As your skills and experience grow, you may wish to invest in more advanced gear to capture even more distant signals.
5. **Practice Patience**: Successful DXing often requires multiple attempts, and not every session will yield a new and exotic catch. Be patient and persistent in your pursuit.

Conclusion

Receiving distant signals on the shortwave bands is a thrilling and rewarding endeavor that allows you to explore the world from the comfort of your listening post. As you continue your journey of shortwave radio mastery, remember that the key to success lies in understanding propagation, employing the right equipment, and honing your techniques.

In the following chapters of "Shortwave Radio Mastery: A Listener's Journey," we'll delve further into the practical aspects of shortwave listening. From decoding various types of broadcasts to optimizing your listening experience, your adventure through the shortwave bands is just beginning. So, tune in, explore, and continue to chase the magic of distant signals.

Continue reading to further your understanding and mastery of shortwave radio, as we explore the practical aspects of tuning in to fascinating broadcasts from across the globe.

6.BEYOND THE AIRWAVES

Digital Modes and Data Reception

Shortwave radio has long been a fascinating medium for radio enthusiasts. With its vast range of frequencies and the ability to capture transmissions from around the world, shortwave radio has been a staple of global communication for decades. In the digital age, the world of shortwave radio has evolved, offering listeners a broader spectrum of experiences and capabilities. One of the most exciting developments in shortwave radio is the use of digital modes and data reception, which have expanded the horizons of what listeners can do and receive. This article explores the fascinating world of digital modes and data reception on shortwave radio and their vital role in the realm of radio enthusiasts.

The Evolution of Shortwave Radio

Shortwave radio, also known as high-frequency (HF) radio, operates on frequencies between 3 and 30 MHz. These frequencies are ideal for long-distance communication because they can travel vast distances by bouncing off the Earth's ionosphere. This characteristic made shortwave radio an invaluable tool for international broadcasting, especially during times when conventional means of communication were unavailable.

In the early days of shortwave radio, it primarily served as a medium for voice broadcasts, and listeners tuned in to listen to news, music, and cultural programs from around the world. These broadcasts often faced interference, fading signals, and static, but the allure of receiving distant transmissions and discovering new cultures made shortwave radio an engaging hobby.

However, as technology progressed and the digital age dawned, the world of shortwave radio evolved. Digital technology brought a new dimension to the hobby, making it possible for enthusiasts to do much more than just listen. The introduction of digital modes and data reception marked a turning point in the history of shortwave radio.

Digital Modes and Data Reception

Digital modes in shortwave radio refer to a variety of techniques that use digital encoding to transmit and receive information. These modes are versatile, allowing radio operators to exchange text, images, and even data files. Digital modes have several advantages over traditional analog voice transmissions, including greater resistance to noise and interference, efficient use of bandwidth, and the ability to transmit and receive data in poor conditions.

Data reception, on the other hand, is the process of capturing and interpreting digital data transmitted via shortwave radio. This data can range from simple text messages to weather images and telemetry data from satellites. Radio enthusiasts can use specialized equipment and software to decode and display this information on their computers, opening up a whole new world of possibilities.

Understanding Digital Modes

To grasp the potential of digital modes on shortwave radio, it's essential to understand how they work. Digital modes use various modulation techniques to encode information for transmission. Some of the most popular digital modes include:

1. **Morse Code (CW - Continuous Wave):** While not a new technology, Morse code remains a popular digital mode among amateur radio operators. It relies on simple on-off keying to represent text using dots and dashes.
2. **RTTY (Radio Teletype):** RTTY is a mode that transmits text by shifting the frequency of the carrier signal for "mark" and "space" signals. It is widely used for news bulletins, weather reports, and amateur radio conversations.

3. **PSK (Phase Shift Keying):** PSK modulates the phase of the carrier signal to represent binary data. It is highly efficient and resistant to interference, making it suitable for weak signal reception.
4. **AMTOR (Amateur Teletype Over Radio):** AMTOR is a robust mode designed for reliable communication under adverse conditions. It can automatically retransmit information if errors occur during reception.
5. **FT8/FT4:** These are part of the family of Weak Signal Propagation Reporting (WSJT) modes and are popular for making contact with weak signals. They are widely used by amateur radio operators for digital communication.
6. **PACTOR:** PACTOR is a versatile mode used for data transmission, particularly for sending emails via shortwave radio. It provides error-checking and automatic repeat requests for reliable data exchange.
7. **SSTV (Slow Scan Television):** SSTV encodes images into an audio signal that can be transmitted over the airwaves. Radio enthusiasts can receive and decode images from other radio operators or even from satellites.
8. **APRS (Automatic Packet Reporting System):** APRS is a digital mode used for real-time tactical digital communications of information of immediate value in the local area. It is commonly used for tracking the positions of amateur radio operators.

These digital modes offer a range of applications and enable shortwave radio enthusiasts to engage in diverse activities, from basic text communication to image and data reception.

Getting Started with Digital Modes

To get started with digital modes on shortwave radio, you'll need some essential equipment and software:

1. **Shortwave Radio Receiver:** You'll need a shortwave radio receiver capable of tuning into the frequencies you intend to monitor. There are various types of receivers, from portable

units to desktop models, with different features and price ranges.

2. **Computer:** A computer is essential for decoding digital modes. It should have an audio input to connect to your receiver and appropriate software for decoding the chosen mode.
3. **Audio Interface:** To connect your receiver to the computer, you'll need an audio interface. This can be as simple as an audio cable with the appropriate connectors or a dedicated USB sound card.
4. **Antenna:** A good antenna can significantly improve your reception. Consider installing an outdoor wire antenna for better results.
5. **Software:** There are numerous software applications available for decoding digital modes. Popular choices include fldigi, MultiPSK, and WSJT-X for modes like FT8 and FT4.
6. **Knowledge:** Familiarize yourself with the chosen digital mode and the software you'll be using. Learning the specific requirements and settings for each mode is essential for successful decoding.

With these tools in place, you can embark on your journey into the world of digital modes on shortwave radio.

Applications of Digital Modes

The versatility of digital modes on shortwave radio opens up a wide range of applications for radio enthusiasts. Let's explore some of the most common and exciting uses of these modes:

1. **Amateur Radio Communication:** Digital modes are widely used in the amateur radio community for long-distance and weak signal communication. Radio operators can exchange messages, make contacts, and participate in contests using digital modes like PSK, RTTY, and FT8.
2. **Weather Monitoring:** Many weather services around the world transmit weather reports and forecasts on shortwave frequencies. These reports often include data on temperature, wind speed, and atmospheric conditions. By decoding these

transmissions, listeners can access real-time weather information for their area or regions of interest.

3. **Maritime and Aviation Communications:** Shortwave radio is still a crucial medium for maritime and aviation communications. Digital modes play a significant role in transmitting navigational information, weather updates, and distress signals.

4. **Utility Stations:** Various utility stations, such as time signals, navigation beacons, and military transmissions, use digital modes to convey information. Radio enthusiasts can receive and decode these transmissions to stay informed or for the sheer pleasure of exploring the hidden world of utility stations.

5. **Space Communications:** Space agencies and amateur radio satellites often transmit telemetry data, images, and even messages on shortwave frequencies. Radio operators can receive and decode these transmissions, making it possible to track satellites, receive images from space, and contribute to citizen science projects.

6. **Emergency Communication:** Digital modes are known for their reliability in adverse conditions. During emergencies, such as natural disasters, amateur radio operators often use digital modes to establish communication networks for emergency services and disaster relief organizations.

7. **DXing:** DXing, the art of listening to distant stations, takes on new dimensions with digital modes. Enthusiasts can search for rare and exotic stations transmitting digital data, expanding the horizons of their listening experience.

8. **Data Decoding Challenges:** Many radio enthusiasts enjoy the challenge of decoding encrypted or coded messages from government agencies, spies, or numbers stations. These activities add an element of mystery and intrigue to the hobby.

By delving into these applications, radio enthusiasts can make the most of digital modes and data reception on shortwave radio and unlock new horizons of exploration.

Enhancing Shortwave Radio Reception

The incorporation of digital modes into shortwave radio has not only expanded the possibilities for radio enthusiasts but has also enhanced the overall reception experience. Here's how:

1. **Improved Signal Quality:** Digital modes are less susceptible to interference and noise compared to analog voice transmissions. This means that even with less-than-ideal reception conditions, you can still decode messages and data.
2. **Automation:** Many digital mode software applications include features for automatic tuning and decoding. This streamlines the process and allows you to focus on the content rather than manual tuning.
3. **Data Storage and Analysis:** With digital modes, you can save decoded data, log your receptions, and analyze the information at your own pace. This is particularly valuable when tracking weather patterns or collecting telemetry data.
4. **Remote Monitoring:** Some enthusiasts set up remote monitoring stations to receive and decode data from other parts of the world, expanding their reach and capturing unique transmissions.
5. **Community and Collaboration:** Many radio enthusiasts gather on online forums and social media to share their experiences, exchange tips, and collaborate on challenging decoding projects. The sense of community adds depth to the hobby.

The Beauty of Shortwave Radio: A Listener's Journey

Shortwave radio has always held a special allure for radio enthusiasts. The ability to receive signals from distant lands and communicate with people around the world has a unique charm. The introduction of digital modes and data reception has brought shortwave radio into the digital age while preserving its enduring appeal.

The journey of a shortwave radio enthusiast is not just about collecting equipment or chasing rare transmissions. It's a journey through time, space, and cultures. It's a journey of exploration and discovery. With digital modes, this journey becomes even more rewarding.

Imagine sitting in your radio shack, headphones on, and listening to a faint signal from a distant station. As you decode the message, you realize it's an image of a satellite passing over the earth, or perhaps a weather report from a remote island. You've just received a piece of the world, and in that moment, you're connected to something larger than yourself.

Shortwave radio enthusiasts often speak of the thrill of the hunt—the excitement of finding a new station or decoding a challenging signal. It's the sense of adventure and the joy of exploration that keeps enthusiasts coming back to their radios, year after year.

Conclusion

Shortwave radio has come a long way from its origins as a voice-only communication medium. The introduction of digital modes and data reception has transformed the hobby, opening up a world of possibilities for radio enthusiasts. From amateur radio communication to weather monitoring, space exploration, and emergency communication, the applications of digital modes on shortwave radio are diverse and exciting.

In the ever-evolving landscape of communication, shortwave radio stands as a bridge between the past and the future. It continues to captivate the hearts and minds of enthusiasts who appreciate the thrill of the hunt, the joy of decoding hidden messages, and the connection to a global community of fellow radio explorers.

As you embark on your journey into the world of shortwave radio and digital modes, remember that it's not just about technology and signals. It's about the beauty of discovery, the magic of distant voices, and the art of connecting with the world, one digital decode at a time. Shortwave radio mastery is a journey worth taking, and the digital age has only added more layers to this captivating experience. So, tune in, decode, and explore the boundless horizons beyond the airwaves.

7.HUNTING FOR RARE DX

QSL Cards and Verifications

S hortwave radio enthusiasts often describe their hobby as a journey, an adventure into the unknown, where the thrill of exploration is as significant as the rewards of discovery. For those who seek to unlock the secrets of distant lands, the pursuit of Rare DX (long-distance or elusive radio signals) is a passion that drives them to push the boundaries of their equipment, knowledge, and patience. One of the most treasured aspects of this journey is the collection of QSL cards and verifications—proof of successful reception and the golden tickets to the world of Shortwave Radio Mastery.

In this article, we delve into the fascinating world of hunting for Rare DX, the pursuit of elusive stations, and the art of collecting QSL cards and verifications. We'll explore the history, significance, and the joy that comes from receiving these tokens of acknowledgment from broadcasters and fellow radio enthusiasts.

The Significance of Rare DX

Rare DX, often referred to as "DXing," is the practice of receiving distant and challenging radio signals, typically from countries or regions far removed from the listener's location. DXers, as they are known, are driven by the desire to capture the exotic and the elusive—to hear the voices of distant lands, experience diverse cultures, and decode transmissions from places most people may never visit.

The thrill of DXing lies in the uncertainty and unpredictability of radio propagation. Signals can be affected by a myriad of factors, including atmospheric conditions, interference, and the time of day. To achieve a successful DX, radio enthusiasts often invest in sophisticated equipment, including high-quality receivers, antennas, and signal processing tools. They also conduct extensive research, studying propagation patterns, schedules, and frequencies, all in pursuit of those rare, exotic stations that appear on their radios only intermittently.

The allure of Rare DX goes beyond the challenge and the technical aspects. It taps into a fundamental human fascination with the unknown and the desire to connect with the world outside one's immediate surroundings. It's a form of virtual exploration that bridges geographical and cultural gaps.

The History of QSL Cards

QSL cards play a central role in the world of DXing. The term "QSL" originates from the radio communication code, where "Q" signals were used to represent specific messages. In this context, "QSL" stands for "confirmation of receipt" or "acknowledgment."

QSL cards, typically postcard-sized, are sent by broadcasters to confirm that a listener successfully received their broadcast. These cards often feature the broadcaster's logo, call sign, and other relevant information. They serve as official documentation and trophies for DXers, certifying their achievement in capturing a specific broadcast.

The tradition of QSL cards in the world of radio dates back to the early days of broadcasting, where listeners would send reception reports (or SWL reports, standing for Shortwave Listening) to radio stations to confirm their successful reception. In return, the stations would send QSL cards, sometimes with personalized messages or additional information about the station and its programming. This exchange created a tangible connection between broadcasters and their global audience.

The evolution of technology and communication methods led to a decline in the use of QSL cards in the broadcasting industry. However, among dedicated DXers, collecting QSL cards remains a cherished practice, preserving a rich tradition and an enduring connection between listener and broadcaster.

The Joy of Collecting QSL Cards

For DXers, collecting QSL cards is more than just a hobby; it's a passion that adds depth to their shortwave radio journey. The joy of collecting QSL cards can be attributed to several key factors:

1. **Validation of Achievements:** QSL cards serve as tangible proof of a DXer's achievements. They represent the successful reception of signals from distant and often challenging stations. Each card carries a story of a connection made through the airwaves.
2. **Cultural Exploration:** QSL cards often include details about the broadcaster's location, culture, and programming. Collecting these cards allows DXers to explore and learn about different regions of the world, often in a way that surpasses what can be found in travel guides.
3. **Connecting with Broadcasters:** Receiving a QSL card from a broadcaster provides a direct connection with the station's staff. It's an acknowledgment of the listener's interest and a validation of their dedication to the hobby.
4. **Historical Significance:** Many QSL cards hold historical value, offering insights into the history of broadcasting and radio technology. Some cards even feature images of iconic radio transmitters and antennas.
5. **Building a Collection:** The act of collecting QSL cards, like any hobby, fosters a sense of accomplishment. DXers take pride in the growth of their collections, with each card representing a unique piece of the puzzle.
6. **Fostering a Sense of Community:** DXing is often a solitary activity, but the exchange of QSL cards forms a sense of community among enthusiasts. Cards can be traded or gifted, creating a network of like-minded individuals.

QSL cards come in a wide variety of designs and styles, reflecting the diversity of broadcasters and the cultures they represent. Some collectors focus on specific themes or regions, while others aim for a diverse and extensive collection. The pursuit of rare or sought-after QSL cards adds an extra layer of excitement to the hobby.

Obtaining QSL Cards

The process of obtaining QSL cards involves several steps, and DXers must be persistent, patient, and resourceful. Here's a general overview of how to secure QSL cards:

1. **Reception Report:** When a DXer successfully receives a broadcast, they send a reception report to the station. This report typically includes details such as the date and time of reception, frequency, program details, and signal strength.
2. **Include Return Postage:** To receive a QSL card, it's common for DXers to include a self-addressed envelope along with return postage. This makes it easy for the broadcaster to send a card in return.
3. **Wait Patiently:** Obtaining QSL cards requires patience. Broadcasters may receive numerous reception reports, and it can take time for them to process and respond to each one.
4. **Follow Up:** If a reasonable amount of time passes without receiving a QSL card, DXers can send a polite follow-up request. This gentle reminder can prompt a response.
5. **Participate in QSL Club Programs:** Many broadcasters and shortwave radio organizations have QSL club programs. DXers can join these clubs, which often offer additional perks, such as newsletters and exclusive QSL cards.
6. **Engage Online Communities:** Online forums, social media groups, and websites dedicated to DXing are valuable resources for connecting with other enthusiasts and learning about broadcasters that issue QSL cards.

The Art of QSL Card Design

QSL cards come in various styles and designs, ranging from simple, utilitarian cards to intricate and artistic creations. The design of a QSL card often reflects the character and identity of the broadcasting station. Here are some elements commonly found on QSL cards:

1. **Station Logo:** The station's logo is typically featured prominently on the card. This logo is often an emblem of the

station's identity and brand.

2. **Call Sign:** The station's call sign is a critical piece of information on the card. It helps confirm the identity of the broadcaster.
3. **Station Information:** QSL cards may include details about the station's history, transmitter location, and the languages they broadcast in.
4. **Program Details:** Some cards provide information about the programs or shows the station airs, allowing listeners to learn more about the station's content.
5. **Photographs or Illustrations:** Many QSL cards feature images that represent the station's culture or the location of its transmitter. These images can be photographs of local landmarks, landscapes, or illustrations of historical figures.
6. **Contact Information:** The card may include contact details for the station, such as an email address, website, or postal address.
7. **Confirmation of Reception:** The card will usually include a statement confirming the listener's reception, sometimes with additional information about the signal quality.
8. **Personalization:** Some broadcasters take the extra step of personalizing QSL cards with the DXer's name and reception details.

The beauty of QSL cards lies in their diversity. Collectors often appreciate the uniqueness of each card and the insights they provide into different cultures and broadcasting traditions. Over the years, QSL card design has evolved, incorporating new technologies and artistic styles while retaining the tradition's spirit.

Online Resources and Communities

In the digital age, the internet has become a powerful tool for DXers and QSL card collectors. Online communities and resources have made it easier to connect with fellow enthusiasts, discover new stations, and exchange QSL cards. Here are some of the valuable online resources for QSL card collectors:

1. **QSL Websites:** There are websites dedicated to cataloging QSL cards and providing information about stations, their schedules, and the availability of QSL cards.
2. **Online Forums:** Online forums and discussion boards related to DXing and shortwave radio are excellent places to connect with like-minded individuals, seek advice, and trade QSL cards.
3. **Social Media:** Social media platforms, particularly Facebook and Twitter, have active communities of DXers and QSL card collectors. Joining relevant groups and following enthusiasts can lead to valuable connections.
4. **QSL Clubs:** Many broadcasters and shortwave radio organizations have QSL clubs with websites and forums for members. These clubs often provide access to exclusive QSL cards and newsletters.
5. **DXing Blogs:** Some DXers maintain blogs or websites where they share their experiences, including reception reports and QSL card collections. These blogs can be inspirational and informative.
6. **Online Logs:** Several websites offer databases of reception reports and QSL cards, allowing collectors to search for specific cards and discover what others have received.

QSL Card Contests and Awards

For many DXers, the pursuit of QSL cards goes beyond simple collection. They may participate in contests and awards programs designed to recognize their achievements. These contests often have specific requirements, such as receiving a certain number of cards from different countries or continents, or capturing signals from rare and elusive stations. The joy of participating in these contests comes not only from the potential awards but also from the thrill of competition and the chance to test one's skills.

Awards programs and contests add an extra layer of excitement to DXing, motivating enthusiasts to explore new territories and push their boundaries. The allure of capturing Rare DX and obtaining coveted QSL cards can be a powerful incentive for DXers to refine their techniques and equipment.

Conclusion

The world of Rare DX, QSL cards, and verifications is a captivating dimension of the shortwave radio journey. It combines elements of adventure, exploration, history, and culture, all within the realm of radio waves. Collecting QSL cards is not merely a hobby; it's a passion that binds radio enthusiasts to the broader community of broadcasters, DXers, and fellow collectors.

In an era when instant communication and digital technologies dominate, the pursuit of Rare DX and the exchange of QSL cards offer a unique connection to a bygone era of radio. It's a reminder that, even in the age of the internet, the world of shortwave radio remains a frontier where the unknown still beckons and distant voices can be heard.

So, whether you are an experienced DXer with a collection of treasured QSL cards or a newcomer to the world of shortwave radio, the pursuit of Rare DX and QSL cards is an opportunity to embark on a journey of discovery, connection, and the thrill of exploring the invisible airwaves. It is a journey that adds depth to the mastery of shortwave radio and a celebration of the enduring allure of the unknown.

8.LISTENING TECHNIQUES

Maximizing Signal Clarity

S hortwave radio, with its ability to capture signals from around the world, is a medium that has captivated radio enthusiasts for generations. The allure of tuning in to distant broadcasts, exploring different cultures, and receiving transmissions from far-off places is a powerful draw. However, the world of shortwave radio is not always a realm of perfect signal clarity. Interference, fading, and noise are common challenges faced by listeners. In this article, we delve into the art of maximizing signal clarity through listening techniques. These techniques can help shortwave radio enthusiasts unlock the full potential of their receivers and enjoy a more rewarding listening experience.

The Importance of Signal Clarity

Signal clarity is a critical aspect of shortwave radio listening. It refers to the quality of the received signal, which includes the strength, stability, and absence of interference or noise. Maximizing signal clarity is essential because it directly impacts the ability to tune in to distant stations, understand broadcasts, and fully appreciate the content.

The challenges to signal clarity in shortwave radio are numerous:

1. **Distance:** Shortwave signals travel vast distances, which can lead to variations in signal strength and reception quality. Factors like the time of day, atmospheric conditions, and the Earth's ionosphere play significant roles in signal propagation.

2. **Interference:** Shortwave bands are crowded with signals from various broadcasters and sources. Adjacent channels often

overlap, causing interference. In addition, electronic devices and man-made radio frequency interference (RFI) contribute to signal degradation.

3. **Fading:** Fading is a phenomenon where the strength of a signal varies rapidly, making it challenging to maintain a stable reception. Fading can be caused by factors like changes in ionospheric conditions and multipath propagation.

4. **Noise:** External sources of noise, such as electrical devices and power lines, can introduce unwanted noise into the signal. Atmospheric noise, including static and lightning, is also common.

Given these challenges, it's essential for shortwave radio enthusiasts to develop techniques and strategies to maximize signal clarity.

Listening Techniques for Signal Clarity

1. **Choose the Right Frequency:** One of the most fundamental listening techniques is choosing the right frequency. Different frequencies are suitable for different times of day and for reaching specific regions. Utilize online resources, frequency guides, and schedules to identify the ideal frequency for your target station.

2. **Use a Quality Receiver:** Investing in a high-quality receiver with good selectivity and sensitivity is paramount. A better receiver will perform more effectively in separating signals and reducing interference. When selecting a receiver, consider the type of shortwave listening you plan to do, whether it's casual tuning or serious DXing.

3. **Optimize Your Antenna:** Your antenna is a crucial component for signal reception. Experiment with different antenna types and configurations to find the setup that works best for your location. Outdoor wire antennas, loop antennas, and long wire antennas are common choices for shortwave listening.

4. **Consider an Antenna Tuner:** An antenna tuner can help match your antenna's impedance to that of your receiver, enhancing signal strength and minimizing interference.

5. **Minimize Electrical Noise:** Electrical devices in your home can introduce noise into your receiver. Turn off or unplug any devices that may be causing interference, such as computers, fluorescent lights, or televisions.

6. **Employ Ferrite Cores:** Attach ferrite cores to your antenna and audio cables to suppress interference. These cores are especially useful in reducing RFI.

7. **Select the Right Time:** Shortwave reception is highly dependent on time. Some frequencies work better during daylight, while others are more active at night. Take time to explore different times of day to discover when your target stations are most accessible.

8. **Understanding Propagation:** Familiarize yourself with the various propagation modes, including groundwave, skywave, and spacewave. Knowing how signals travel can help you predict when and where to listen.

9. **Experiment with Antenna Placement:** The location of your antenna matters. Elevating it, using an outdoor antenna, or moving it away from sources of interference can significantly improve signal clarity.

10. **Use a Noise-Reducing Headset:** A good-quality noise-reducing headset can help you concentrate on the signal and reduce background noise, providing a clearer audio experience.

11. **Learn Morse Code (CW):** Morse code transmissions (CW) are among the most robust signals on shortwave. Learning Morse code allows you to decipher signals even when the audio is barely audible.

12. **Digital Noise Reduction (DNR):** Some modern shortwave receivers are equipped with digital noise reduction technology that can effectively reduce background noise. Experiment with these features to see if they improve signal clarity.

13. **Tune Carefully:** Use a slow and steady tuning technique to minimize interference from adjacent channels. Listen for signals that are just above or below the noise level and fine-tune to improve clarity.

14. **Use Synchronous Detection:** Many shortwave receivers have synchronous detection features that can help lock onto a signal and reduce interference. Experiment with this feature to see if it improves reception.
15. **Preselector Filters:** If your receiver has preselector filters, use them to narrow down the bandwidth and reduce interference from nearby signals.
16. **Filter Settings:** Adjust the bandwidth and filter settings on your receiver to isolate the signal you want to hear. Narrowing the bandwidth can help eliminate adjacent channel interference.
17. **Use AGC (Automatic Gain Control):** AGC can help maintain a constant audio level, reducing the impact of signal fading. Experiment with different AGC settings to find the most suitable one for your listening conditions.
18. **Learn the Language of Numbers Stations:** Numbers stations are enigmatic transmissions used for espionage and intelligence purposes. Learning how to identify and decode these signals can add a layer of intrigue to your shortwave listening.
19. **Participate in DX Contests:** Participating in DX contests and events can be an enjoyable way to test your listening skills and engage with other enthusiasts. These contests often provide the opportunity to chase after elusive stations.
20. **Join Online Communities:** There are numerous online forums, social media groups, and websites dedicated to shortwave radio enthusiasts. These communities can be excellent sources of tips, advice, and information about listening conditions.
21. **QSL Cards and Verifications:** Receiving QSL cards and verifications from stations can be rewarding. These cards not only serve as trophies but also as acknowledgment of your reception success. Many broadcasters appreciate reception reports and are happy to send QSL cards in return.

By combining these listening techniques and strategies, you can significantly enhance your ability to receive shortwave radio signals with clarity, making your listening experience more rewarding and enjoyable.

Chasing Rare DX

One of the most exciting aspects of shortwave radio is the pursuit of Rare DX—those elusive and exotic stations that challenge the limits of your equipment and listening skills. DXing is a rewarding and thrilling dimension of shortwave radio listening, and achieving success in this endeavor often requires the application of advanced listening techniques.

Here are some additional strategies to help you chase after Rare DX:

1. **Stay Informed:** Keep yourself updated on current propagation conditions, including solar activity and geomagnetic indices. This knowledge can help you anticipate when certain stations may become accessible.
2. **Seek Out Scheduled Special Broadcasts:** Some stations, especially those aimed at an international audience, schedule special broadcasts for significant events or holidays. These can be excellent opportunities to hear unusual or rare content.
3. **Listen During Sporadic E and Meteor Scatter Events:** These atmospheric conditions can result in signal propagation that allows you to receive stations outside your normal range.
4. **Explore Unconventional Bands:** While the majority of shortwave broadcasts fall within the standard HF bands, some stations operate outside these bands. Explore unconventional frequencies to discover hidden gems.
5. **Master Your Receiver's Features:** Learn how to use your receiver's features effectively. Experiment with different modes, filters, and tuning methods to maximize your reception capabilities.
6. **Build a Comprehensive Shortwave Library:** Collect frequency guides, propagation charts, and station schedules. These resources will help you plan your listening sessions and target specific stations.
7. **Participate in DX Contests and Events:** Joining contests and events can sharpen your skills and introduce you to stations you might not encounter otherwise.
8. **Connect with Other DXers:** Building relationships with fellow DXers can be invaluable. They can share their experiences and

knowledge, and you can learn from their successes and challenges.

9. **Employ Remote SDRs:** Consider using remote software-defined radios (SDRs) to access receivers in other parts of the world. This can expand your listening range and open up opportunities to hear stations you may never have encountered otherwise.

The pursuit of Rare DX is a rewarding aspect of shortwave radio listening, requiring a blend of technical expertise, dedication, and the application of advanced listening techniques. Whether it's hearing a station from a remote island, capturing an exotic language, or receiving a transmission from a seldom-heard region, achieving Rare DX is a testament to the listener's skills and the thrill of the radio journey.

9. BROADCASTS FROM AROUND THE GLOBE

Cultural Discovery

Shortwave radio is a gateway to the world. It transcends borders, traverses oceans, and connects people across vast distances. For radio enthusiasts, it's a medium that offers much more than just music and news. Shortwave radio is a powerful tool for cultural discovery, a window through which we can explore the rich tapestry of the world's cultures, languages, and traditions. In this article, we embark on a journey of cultural exploration through the broadcasts from around the globe. We'll delve into the transformative power of shortwave radio and the role it plays in broadening our horizons and fostering cross-cultural understanding.

The Global Tapestry of Shortwave Radio

Shortwave radio, also known as high-frequency (HF) radio, operates on frequencies between 3 and 30 MHz. These frequencies allow radio signals to travel long distances by reflecting off the Earth's ionosphere. This unique characteristic has made shortwave radio a vital tool for international broadcasting, and it has played a significant role in connecting people around the world.

Every day, hundreds of broadcasters transmit their signals into the ether, reaching audiences on distant continents. These broadcasts include news, music, cultural programs, religious services, and much more. The diversity of content is matched only by the diversity of the people who create it and the listeners who tune in.

The global tapestry of shortwave radio is woven with threads of culture, language, and identity. For listeners, this medium is a means to explore and connect with cultures far removed from their own, fostering a sense of global citizenship and understanding. Shortwave radio is a passport to a world of discovery.

The Power of Language

Language is the key to unlocking the cultural riches of shortwave radio. Every language is a window into a unique way of life, a portal into the heart of a culture. Shortwave radio provides access to broadcasts in languages spoken by people around the world, from Swahili to Spanish, Arabic to Zulu. Each language carries the essence of a culture, and by listening to broadcasts in different languages, we can immerse ourselves in the traditions, stories, and perspectives of others.

Shortwave radio broadcasts in native languages are a bridge between listeners and the people of a particular region. By tuning in, we can experience the vibrancy of languages spoken daily in homes, marketplaces, and neighborhoods halfway across the world. We become honorary citizens, if only for a few moments, as we listen to the rhythms and cadences of spoken words in languages we may never fully understand.

In addition to serving as a linguistic portal, shortwave radio also offers language learners a valuable resource for improving their skills. Listening to authentic language use in real-world contexts is an effective way to enhance language proficiency. Furthermore, it's a reminder of the interconnectedness of the world, where communication transcends linguistic boundaries.

Cultural Programs and Insights

Shortwave radio broadcasts encompass a vast array of cultural programs that provide insight into the traditions, history, and daily life of various communities. These programs offer a glimpse into the heart of a culture, providing listeners with a greater understanding of the world's diversity. Here are some of the cultural programs you might encounter while exploring shortwave radio:

1. **Music:** Music is a universal language, and it's a prominent feature of shortwave radio broadcasts. Listeners can tune in to music from every corner of the globe, from the hypnotic

rhythms of African drumming to the intricate melodies of classical Indian ragas. Each region has its musical traditions that express the hopes, dreams, and emotions of its people.

2. **Cultural Heritage:** Broadcasts often delve into the cultural heritage of a region, offering stories, folklore, and historical accounts that reveal the roots of a culture. These programs are like guided tours through the annals of history, allowing listeners to understand the collective memory of a people.

3. **Religion:** Shortwave radio is a platform for religious broadcasts from various faiths, including Christianity, Islam, Buddhism, Hinduism, and more. These programs provide spiritual insights and rituals from different parts of the world, promoting understanding and tolerance among different religious communities.

4. **Cooking and Cuisine:** Cultural programs often explore the culinary traditions of a region. Listeners can learn about local ingredients, cooking techniques, and traditional recipes. These programs offer a taste of the flavors that define a culture.

5. **Literature:** Literary programs feature readings, discussions, and analyses of classic and contemporary works. They provide a window into a culture's storytelling traditions, with a focus on the themes and narratives that resonate with a people.

6. **Arts and Crafts:** Some broadcasts feature the visual arts, craft traditions, and artistic expressions of a culture. These programs offer insights into the creativity and craftsmanship that shape a community's identity.

7. **Festivals and Celebrations:** Cultural broadcasts often highlight the festivals and celebrations that are central to a culture's calendar. Listeners can experience the joy, music, and rituals that define these special occasions.

8. **Language Lessons:** Language learners can benefit from broadcasts that offer language lessons, allowing them to acquire a basic understanding of a new language.

The Role of International Broadcasting

International broadcasters play a crucial role in cultural exchange and understanding through shortwave radio. These broadcasters, often affiliated with governments or private organizations, transmit their content worldwide, aiming to reach global audiences. Their mission goes beyond simply disseminating information; they act as cultural ambassadors, sharing the traditions, values, and stories of their respective nations.

One of the most iconic international broadcasters is the BBC World Service, known for its high-quality journalism and cultural programming. The Voice of America, Radio Free Europe/Radio Liberty, and Deutsche Welle are also influential in the world of international broadcasting. These broadcasters cover a broad range of topics and maintain a diverse lineup of programs designed to engage audiences around the world.

Cultural exchange programs, in particular, are an essential element of international broadcasting. They allow listeners to discover the customs, art, and heritage of other countries. These programs contribute to mutual respect and appreciation of different cultures, fostering cross-cultural dialogue.

The Importance of Community Radio

While international broadcasters serve as cultural ambassadors on a global scale, community radio stations play a more localized, grassroots role in cultural preservation and exchange. Community radio stations, often operated by volunteers and community members, are dedicated to preserving and promoting the culture, language, and traditions of a specific region or community.

These stations focus on local issues and cultural preservation, offering an authentic representation of the community's values and heritage. By listening to community radio stations on shortwave, you can gain a deeper understanding of regional cultures and the challenges they face.

Community radio programs often focus on the following aspects of cultural exchange:

1. **Language Preservation:** In many parts of the world, indigenous languages are at risk of extinction. Community radio

stations provide a platform for the preservation and revitalization of these languages.

2. **Folklore and Traditions:** These programs celebrate folklore, oral traditions, and cultural practices that are central to the identity of a community.
3. **Music and Dance:** Folk music, traditional instruments, and dance are celebrated through radio broadcasts, allowing listeners to immerse themselves in the sounds of a community.
4. **Cultural Dialogues:** Community radio stations foster dialogue about cultural identity, heritage, and the challenges facing a community. These dialogues often include input from community members.

Cultural exchanges facilitated by community radio are vital for the preservation of indigenous knowledge and traditions. They enable listeners to engage with the intimate aspects of a culture, gaining insights into the lives, values, and aspirations of a particular community.

Digital Shortwave Radio and Cultural Discovery

In recent years, advancements in technology have expanded the ways in which listeners can explore cultures through shortwave radio. The emergence of digital shortwave radio has brought improvements in signal quality, audio fidelity, and ease of tuning. This has made the reception of shortwave broadcasts even more accessible and enjoyable for enthusiasts.

Digital modes, such as Digital Radio Mondiale (DRM), have introduced a new era of audio clarity and reduced interference on shortwave. DRM broadcasts can provide near-FM quality audio, which is particularly advantageous for programs featuring music, interviews, and cultural insights.

Online SDRs (Software-Defined Radios) have become an increasingly popular tool for shortwave radio enthusiasts. These platforms allow users to remotely access and control shortwave receivers located in different parts of the world. It means that, from the comfort of your computer or mobile device, you can tune in to shortwave broadcasts from various regions, exploring cultural programs, languages, and music from around the globe.

Online communities, forums, and social media groups dedicated to shortwave radio have created a virtual space for enthusiasts to share their discoveries and exchange insights into cultural broadcasts. Listeners often exchange tips on which frequencies to tune in to for specific cultural content, making it easier to explore and engage with the diversity of shortwave radio programming.

The Thrill of Cultural Discovery

The journey of cultural discovery through shortwave radio is a thrilling experience. It's a journey that unfolds in the intimate space of your listening environment, where you become an explorer, venturing into different worlds through the airwaves. Here are some of the thrills that come with cultural discovery:

1. **Experiencing New Sounds:** Each culture has its unique sounds and rhythms. Through shortwave radio, you can immerse yourself in the sounds of different regions, from the haunting melodies of Middle Eastern music to the energetic beats of Latin American rhythms.
2. **Language Learning:** Listening to broadcasts in foreign languages is not only a way to discover culture but also a path to language learning. Understanding and appreciating the nuances of different languages can be a rewarding experience.
3. **Connecting with People:** Shortwave radio enables you to connect with people from around the world. When you listen to a program that resonates with you, you're connecting with individuals who share similar interests and values, even if you may never meet them in person.
4. **Experiencing Traditions:** Cultural broadcasts often feature traditional stories, rituals, and customs. Listening to these programs is like receiving a personal invitation to participate in the traditions of a community.
5. **Strengthening Cross-Cultural Understanding:** Cultural discovery through shortwave radio fosters cross-cultural understanding and appreciation. It allows you to step into the shoes of others and view the world through their eyes.

6. **Exploring the Uncharted:** Shortwave radio is an exploration of the unknown. When you discover a new broadcast or a unique cultural program, you're embarking on a journey of exploration and discovery.

Conclusion

Shortwave radio is a remarkable medium that transcends geographical boundaries and connects people across the globe. Through the broadcasts from around the world, listeners can embark on a journey of cultural discovery that is both enriching and transformative. The power of shortwave radio lies in its ability to bring the world to your doorstep, allowing you to explore languages, traditions, music, and values that may be vastly different from your own.

Cultural discovery through shortwave radio is a testament to the enduring role of this medium in fostering cross-cultural understanding and appreciation. It reminds us that the world is a diverse tapestry of cultures, each with its unique stories, languages, and perspectives. Shortwave radio is the passport to this world of discovery, and it invites us to embark on a lifelong journey of exploration, one broadcast at a time.

10.EMERGENCY COMMUNICATIONS

Shortwave Radio in Times of Crisis

I n a world marked by technological advancements, instant communication, and the pervasive use of smartphones, one might wonder about the relevance of shortwave radio. While it is true that shortwave radio has taken a back seat in many aspects of our lives, it remains a vital tool for one critical function: emergency communication. In times of crisis, whether caused by natural disasters, political unrest, or unforeseen emergencies, shortwave radio has proven itself to be a lifeline. When other means of communication falter or become overwhelmed, shortwave radio offers a reliable and resilient channel for receiving and transmitting critical information. This article explores the invaluable role of shortwave radio in emergency communications, the history of its use in times of crisis, and the ongoing relevance of this technology in our rapidly changing world.

A Lifeline in Crisis

Emergencies can strike at any time, and they often bring with them chaos, disruption, and confusion. Whether it's a devastating earthquake, a hurricane, a power outage, or a civil unrest, access to accurate and timely information is crucial for survival and recovery. Shortwave radio, with its unique properties, has been a trusted tool for emergency communication, offering several advantages in such situations:

1. **Global Reach:** Shortwave radio signals can travel vast distances, often circumventing local infrastructure issues that other communication methods may face. This global reach ensures that critical information can be received from sources far beyond the affected area.
2. **Independence from Local Infrastructure:** Shortwave radio is not reliant on local infrastructure, such as cell towers or internet connectivity. It operates independently, making it less vulnerable to damage or disruption.
3. **Redundancy:** Shortwave radio serves as a redundancy in communication networks. When other systems fail, it can continue to operate, providing a backup channel for essential information flow.
4. **Low Cost:** Shortwave radios are relatively affordable and do not require a subscription or network access fees. They can be essential tools for communities with limited resources.
5. **Battery-Powered:** Shortwave radios can be operated using batteries, solar power, or hand-cranked generators, making them suitable for use when the electrical grid is down.
6. **Versatility:** Shortwave radios can receive a wide range of transmissions, from amateur radio operators to government emergency services. This versatility ensures access to a diverse range of information sources.

The History of Shortwave Radio in Emergencies

The use of shortwave radio in times of crisis dates back to the early days of the technology. Here are some historical examples of its pivotal role in emergency communications:

1. **World War II:** Shortwave radio played a critical role during World War II, providing a means for governments, resistance movements, and spies to communicate across enemy lines. It was instrumental in coordinating efforts and sharing intelligence.
2. **Natural Disasters:** Shortwave radio has been a lifeline in the aftermath of natural disasters, such as hurricanes, earthquakes,

and tsunamis. Organizations like Radio Amateurs in Civil Emergency Service (RACES) and the Amateur Radio Emergency Service (ARES) have utilized shortwave radio to establish emergency communication networks.

3. **Political Unrest:** In regions experiencing political unrest or censorship, shortwave radio has been a reliable source of uncensored information. During the Arab Spring, for example, shortwave radio played a crucial role in disseminating information and coordinating efforts.

4. **Humanitarian Crises:** Non-governmental organizations (NGOs) and humanitarian agencies often rely on shortwave radio to establish communication in regions affected by humanitarian crises, such as refugee camps and conflict zones.

5. **Remote Areas:** Shortwave radio is vital for remote areas where traditional communication infrastructure is limited or nonexistent. It enables residents to stay connected with the outside world and access vital information.

6. **Maritime and Aviation:** Shortwave radio is crucial for maritime and aviation communication. In emergencies, such as shipwrecks or plane crashes, it can be the primary means of distress calls and coordination of rescue efforts.

Today's Relevance in Modern Emergencies

The importance of shortwave radio in emergencies has not diminished in the digital age; in fact, its role has evolved and expanded. Here's how shortwave radio remains relevant in modern emergencies:

1. **Disaster Preparedness:** Shortwave radio is a valuable tool for disaster preparedness. Preppers, survivalists, and emergency response organizations often include shortwave radios in their preparedness kits. These radios ensure that crucial information can be received when primary communication channels are disrupted.

2. **Weather Warnings:** Shortwave radio broadcasts are frequently used to disseminate weather warnings and information. Organizations like the National Oceanic and Atmospheric

Administration (NOAA) transmit weather reports, including severe weather alerts, on shortwave frequencies.

3. **Public Safety Communications:** Shortwave radio is used by various public safety agencies, including police, fire, and emergency medical services, for communication during crises. It provides an independent communication channel that can be invaluable in emergencies.

4. **International Aid and Relief:** Humanitarian organizations, during international aid missions and relief efforts, utilize shortwave radio to establish communication networks. This technology ensures that aid workers can coordinate and relay vital information in regions with limited infrastructure.

5. **Remote and Isolated Communities:** In remote and isolated areas, shortwave radio remains the primary means of communication. It connects residents to emergency services, medical assistance, and the outside world in times of need.

6. **Community Radio:** Community radio stations often have a presence on shortwave frequencies. These stations serve as hubs for disseminating local information during emergencies, ensuring that communities receive updates and instructions.

7. **Search and Rescue:** Shortwave radio is vital in search and rescue operations. It allows for the coordination of efforts, communication with survivors, and distress calls.

8. **Amateur Radio Operators (HAM):** Amateur radio operators, or "Hams," have a long history of providing emergency communication services. They have established networks and protocols for relaying messages during crises.

9. **Global Connectivity:** Shortwave radio is a means of maintaining global connectivity in emergencies. It can be used to relay messages to international organizations, governments, and news agencies, ensuring that the world is informed about unfolding events.

Challenges and Limitations

While shortwave radio is a powerful tool for emergency communication, it does have some limitations and challenges:

1. **Propagation Conditions:** Shortwave radio signals are influenced by atmospheric conditions, which can lead to fading and variations in signal strength. This may affect the reliability of communication.
2. **Interference:** Shortwave bands are crowded with signals, which can result in interference. It can be challenging to find clear frequencies during times of high demand.
3. **Complexity:** Operating a shortwave radio requires some knowledge of frequencies, propagation, and radio etiquette. This complexity may be a barrier for individuals who are not familiar with the technology.
4. **Equipment Availability:** While shortwave radios are relatively affordable, they may not be readily available in all regions. Access to radios may be limited in areas with low economic resources.
5. **Language Barriers:** The language of broadcasts may present a challenge for some listeners. Understanding foreign languages may be difficult, especially in high-stress situations.
6. **Power Supply:** Shortwave radios require a power source, which may become a limitation in prolonged emergencies where power sources are disrupted.

Preparing for Emergencies with Shortwave Radio

For those interested in harnessing the power of shortwave radio in times of crisis, it's essential to be well-prepared. Here are some steps to consider:

1. **Acquire a Shortwave Radio:** Purchase a reliable shortwave radio with good reception capabilities. Ensure that it can operate on different power sources, including batteries and solar power.
2. **Learn Basic Radio Operation:** Familiarize yourself with your radio's functions and features. Understand how to tune to different frequencies, adjust the antenna, and optimize reception.
3. **Pre-program Frequencies:** Pre-program relevant frequencies, such as weather reports, emergency services, and local

community stations, into your radio for quick access.

4. **Understand Propagation:** Learn about the basics of shortwave propagation, which can help you anticipate when and where to find reliable signals.
5. **Join Amateur Radio Networks:** If possible, become a licensed amateur radio operator (HAM). Amateur radio networks are often essential for relaying messages during emergencies.
6. **Create an Emergency Communication Plan:** Develop a communication plan for emergencies. Define how you will use shortwave radio to stay connected with family, friends, and emergency services.
7. **Gather Emergency Information:** Keep information about emergency frequencies, contacts, and local regulations in your emergency kit. This information will be invaluable in times of crisis.
8. **Practice Regularly:** Regularly practice using your shortwave radio. This includes tuning to different frequencies, sending and receiving messages, and understanding how to maintain your equipment.
9. **Maintain Power Sources:** Ensure that you have a reliable power source for your radio. This may involve having spare batteries, a solar charger, or a hand-crank generator.
10. **Stay Informed:** Stay informed about your region's emergency plans and local frequencies. Ensure that you know where to find official emergency information.
11. **Connect with Local Community Radio:** Establish connections with local community radio stations that broadcast on shortwave frequencies. They may be crucial sources of information during local emergencies.

Shortwave Radio: A Time-Tested Lifeline

Shortwave radio's history of service in emergencies is a testament to its resilience and importance. In times of crisis, when other communication channels may be disrupted, overloaded, or compromised, shortwave radio stands as a reliable and independent source of information and connectivity.

It bridges the gaps between affected regions and the rest of the world, offering a lifeline for those in need.

As we continue to advance in technology, the role of shortwave radio in emergencies remains as vital as ever. It complements modern communication systems and serves as a robust backup, ensuring that critical information flows even when all other channels are impaired. Shortwave radio's global reach, independence from local infrastructure, and versatility make it an invaluable tool for emergency preparedness and response.

The listener's journey through shortwave radio mastery extends beyond the thrill of exploration and the appreciation of diverse cultures. It encompasses the responsibility of being prepared to serve as a communication lifeline when disaster strikes. In the face of crises, shortwave radio is not just a receiver; it is a beacon of hope and a lifeline for those who rely on it for vital information, comfort, and connection.

11.COMMUNITY OF LISTENERS

Joining Clubs and Forums

S hortwave radio listening is a solitary pursuit that takes you on a journey across the airwaves, connecting you to diverse cultures, languages, and stories from around the world. However, despite its solitary nature, shortwave radio listening is not a solitary hobby. It's a passion that has attracted a global community of listeners who share a common love for exploring the radio spectrum. In this article, we explore the importance of joining shortwave radio clubs and forums. These communities provide a sense of belonging, opportunities for learning and collaboration, and the chance to share your passion for shortwave radio with like-minded enthusiasts.

The Loneliness of the Shortwave Listener

Listening to shortwave radio often conjures an image of a solitary listener hunched over a radio receiver, slowly tuning the dial to explore a vast array of signals from around the world. It's a serene and often meditative experience, allowing you to escape the cacophony of everyday life and immerse yourself in the mysteries of distant broadcasts.

However, as much as shortwave listening is a solitary activity, it doesn't have to be a lonely one. The beauty of shortwave radio is that it connects you to a broader world filled with passionate enthusiasts, and joining shortwave radio clubs and forums is the key to unlocking this vibrant community.

The Power of Connection

Shortwave radio enthusiasts are united by a shared fascination with the medium's endless possibilities. They gather to discuss their latest reception reports, exchange tips on capturing elusive stations, and share their excitement for their favorite broadcasts. This sense of connection, even in a hobby often characterized by solitude, is a testament to the power of shared interests and the importance of community.

Here are some of the benefits of joining shortwave radio clubs and forums:

1. **Learning Opportunities:** Shortwave radio can be a complex and technically challenging hobby, and it's impossible to know everything there is to know about it. Clubs and forums provide a platform for learning from experienced enthusiasts who can offer guidance, insights, and tips on improving your reception skills.

2. **Sharing Knowledge:** If you've discovered an effective technique for reducing interference or found a unique way to receive a particular station, you can share your knowledge with the community. By contributing to discussions, you become a valuable resource to others.

3. **Exploring New Horizons:** Shortwave radio enthusiasts often have their favorite stations and bands, but joining a community can expose you to new frequencies, broadcasters, and regions you might not have explored otherwise.

4. **Staying Informed:** In the ever-changing world of shortwave radio, staying informed about schedule changes, new stations, and unique broadcasts can be challenging. Clubs and forums are excellent sources of up-to-date information.

5. **Overcoming Challenges:** Shortwave radio listening comes with its fair share of challenges, from interference and fading to antenna issues. When you encounter difficulties, the community can provide solutions and troubleshooting advice.

6. **Reception Reports and Verifications:** Many shortwave radio enthusiasts enjoy receiving QSL cards and verifications from stations they've tuned in to. Clubs often provide guidelines and

templates for sending reception reports and collecting these treasured verifications.

7. **Participating in Contests and Events:** Many shortwave radio clubs organize contests and events that challenge listeners to receive specific stations or engage in themed listening sessions. These events can be fun and educational.

The Vibrant World of Shortwave Radio Clubs

Shortwave radio clubs are communities of enthusiasts who share their love for the medium and collaborate to further the hobby. Here are some notable shortwave radio clubs and organizations from around the world:

1. **North American Shortwave Association (NASWA):** NASWA is one of the oldest and most well-known shortwave radio clubs. They publish a monthly journal and provide a platform for enthusiasts to share their listening experiences.
2. **Worldwide DX Club:** This German-based club connects shortwave listeners from around the world. They publish the popular "DX Window" magazine, and members share their reception reports, loggings, and experiences.
3. **Association of Caversham Transmitters (ACT):** ACT focuses on the historic caversham shortwave transmitting station and preserves the history of broadcasting in Western Australia.
4. **Amateur Radio Relay League (ARRL):** While primarily focused on amateur radio, the ARRL offers resources for shortwave enthusiasts, particularly through its publications and forums.
5. **European DX Council (EDXC):** This organization unites European DX clubs and individual DXers. They organize annual conferences and promote cooperation among European listeners.
6. **South East Asia DXing Club (SEADX):** SEADX is a club dedicated to shortwave and medium wave DXing in Southeast Asia. They offer a quarterly bulletin and encourage the exchange of logs and information among members.

7. **Southgate Amateur Radio Club:** While primarily focused on amateur radio, the Southgate Amateur Radio Club also covers shortwave broadcasting and is an excellent resource for enthusiasts in the UK and beyond.

Online Forums and Communities

In addition to traditional clubs, many shortwave radio enthusiasts congregate in online forums and communities. These digital spaces provide a convenient and accessible way to connect with like-minded individuals from around the world. Some of the most popular online shortwave radio forums and communities include:

1. **DXing.com:** DXing.com is a comprehensive resource for shortwave radio enthusiasts. Their forums cover a wide range of topics, from propagation to specific broadcasters.
2. **The Shortwave Radio Audio Archive:** This website offers a vast collection of shortwave radio audio recordings. Enthusiasts can explore the site's forums to discuss their favorite broadcasts and share their own audio files.
3. **Reddit's Shortwave Listening Community:** Reddit hosts a shortwave radio subreddit where users can share reception reports, seek advice, and engage in discussions about the hobby.
4. **DX World:** DX World is a global resource for radio enthusiasts. Their website features news, articles, and a community forum for listeners to connect and share information.
5. **Utility DXers Forum:** If you're interested in utility stations (e.g., military, aviation, and maritime), this forum is a valuable resource for exchanging information, schedules, and logs.
6. **RadioReference.com:** While primarily focused on public safety radio, RadioReference's forums include sections on shortwave listening and scanner radios. It's an excellent platform for those interested in monitoring various bands.
7. **eHam.net:** eHam.net is a broad resource for amateur radio, but it includes forums and reviews that are relevant to shortwave listeners.

8. **Facebook Groups:** There are numerous Facebook groups dedicated to shortwave radio listening. These groups provide a platform for enthusiasts to connect and discuss the latest happenings in the world of shortwave.

The Etiquette of Online Forums

Online forums and communities offer a wealth of information and interaction, but they also come with their own etiquette and best practices. Here are some guidelines to keep in mind when participating in online shortwave radio forums:

1. **Be Respectful:** Treat fellow members with respect and courtesy. Disagreements can happen, but maintain a civil tone in discussions.
2. **Stay On Topic:** When posting in a forum, keep your contributions relevant to the discussion. If you have a new topic to introduce, consider starting a new thread.
3. **Contribute Positively:** Share your knowledge and experiences to benefit the community. Encourage and support others in their shortwave radio pursuits.
4. **Avoid Self-Promotion:** While it's acceptable to share your own experiences and findings, avoid excessive self-promotion or commercial advertising.
5. **Cite Sources:** When providing information, back it up with sources or references when necessary. This adds credibility to your contributions.
6. **Respect Privacy:** Do not share personal information about others without their consent. Protect your own privacy by refraining from sharing sensitive data.
7. **Observe Forum Rules:** Every forum may have its specific set of rules and guidelines. Familiarize yourself with these rules and adhere to them.

The Quest for Rare DX

Shortwave radio enthusiasts often embark on the quest for Rare DX, which involves capturing the transmissions of distant, uncommon, and hard-to-receive stations. Joining clubs and forums can be particularly advantageous for Rare DX hunters. Here's how these communities can enhance the quest for Rare DX:

1. **Network of Spotters:** Enthusiasts within clubs and forums often share information about rare and unique broadcasts they've encountered. These reports serve as valuable leads for others seeking to capture the same station.
2. **Coordination for Contests:** Many DX clubs and online forums organize contests and events that challenge participants to receive specific, often elusive, stations. These contests offer opportunities to win recognition and awards for Rare DX achievements.
3. **Experienced Advice:** Seasoned DXers in clubs and forums are well-versed in the art of chasing Rare DX. They can provide valuable advice, tips, and techniques for enhancing reception capabilities.
4. **Sharing of Logs:** Many enthusiasts maintain detailed logs of their receptions, including dates, times, frequencies, and station details. These logs can be invaluable for comparing reception conditions and identifying the best times to tune in for Rare DX.
5. **QSL Verification Exchange:** For those seeking QSL cards and verifications from stations, clubs and forums often have sections dedicated to QSL exchange. This is an excellent way to expand your collection of verifications.
6. **Collective Efforts:** Rare DX often requires patience and collective efforts. Enthusiasts may collaborate on scheduling listening sessions, pooling their knowledge and resources to capture elusive stations.

The Rewards of Building a Community

The camaraderie of shortwave radio clubs and forums extends far beyond the reception of distant signals. These communities are built on shared experiences, mutual support, and a passion for exploring the airwaves. By becoming a part of this community, you gain more than just technical knowledge; you gain friends, mentors, and a sense of belonging.

Here are some of the intangible rewards of building a community within the realm of shortwave radio:

1. **Friendships:** The connections made in shortwave radio clubs and forums can lead to lifelong friendships. Enthusiasts from different corners of the world often find common ground and share a sense of camaraderie.
2. **Mentorship:** Seasoned DXers are often willing to mentor newcomers, passing on their knowledge and guiding them in their shortwave radio journeys.
3. **Inspiration:** Being part of a community can be highly motivating. You're exposed to the achievements and enthusiasm of others, which can inspire you to explore new frequencies, refine your skills, and set personal goals.
4. **A Sense of Belonging:** Whether you're a newcomer or a seasoned listener, being part of a community makes you feel like you're part of something larger than yourself. You share in the achievements and discoveries of fellow enthusiasts.
5. **Collaboration:** Community members often collaborate on projects, share equipment, and work together on collective listening efforts. This collaborative spirit can result in shared successes and achievements.
6. **Support:** In times of difficulty or frustration, fellow enthusiasts offer support and encouragement. Whether you're facing interference or struggling to receive a challenging station, the community is there to help.
7. **Preserving the Hobby:** By joining a club or forum, you contribute to the preservation and growth of the shortwave radio hobby. These communities foster interest in shortwave radio and introduce new generations to the magic of radio waves.

Conclusion

Shortwave radio listening is a voyage of exploration and discovery, but it's not a journey meant to be traveled alone. The joy of tuning in to broadcasts from distant lands, the satisfaction of capturing Rare DX, and the sense of wonder in exploring the airwaves are all experiences magnified when shared with a community of like-minded enthusiasts.

Joining shortwave radio clubs and forums is a gateway to this vibrant world of connections and camaraderie. It's an opportunity to learn from experts, inspire newcomers, and become part of a global network of listeners who are passionate about the magic of shortwave radio. So, whether you're a newcomer to the hobby or a seasoned DXer, consider taking the next step in your listener's journey by becoming part of the community of shortwave radio enthusiasts. Together, you'll continue to explore the mysteries of the airwaves and share in the boundless joy of radio listening.

12. ADVENTURES IN THE ETHER

DX-peditions and Expeditions

Shortwave radio listening is an enthralling journey that transports you to distant lands, cultures, and conversations, all through the magic of radio waves. While most shortwave enthusiasts engage in this hobby from the comfort of their homes, others take their passion to a higher level by embarking on DX-peditions and expeditions. These adventures in the ether are the heart of shortwave radio mastery, offering experiences that go beyond the confines of a living room. In this article, we'll delve into the world of DX-peditions and expeditions, exploring what they entail, the allure they hold, and the unforgettable encounters that await those who dare to venture into the vast expanse of the shortwave ether.

The Quest for Elusive Signals

Every shortwave radio enthusiast understands the thrill of tuning in to a distant station and the joy of receiving verifications, also known as QSL cards, from broadcasters. DX-peditions and expeditions take this thrill to a whole new level. The primary goal of these radio adventures is to capture elusive signals from locations far removed from the listener's home.

What distinguishes DX-peditions from regular shortwave listening is the deliberate and often challenging effort made to receive specific stations. Enthusiasts often travel to remote or exotic locations, equipped with specialized gear and knowledge of propagation conditions, to capture the signals of distant stations. These expeditions are not mere vacations; they are meticulously planned quests to uncover radio treasures that lie hidden in the ether.

The Elements of DX-Peditions and Expeditions

DX-peditions and expeditions involve several key elements that distinguish them from casual shortwave listening:

1. **Location, Location, Location:** The choice of location is crucial to the success of a DX-pedition or expedition. Enthusiasts seek areas with minimal interference, low noise levels, and favorable propagation conditions. Remote islands, mountainous regions, or isolated deserts are popular choices.
2. **Specialized Equipment:** DX-peditions require specific equipment tailored for the endeavor. This includes high-performance antennas, portable receivers, amplifiers, and filters designed to maximize reception capabilities.
3. **Proprietary Knowledge:** Successful DXers possess an in-depth understanding of propagation, solar conditions, and geographical influences. They use this knowledge to predict when specific stations will be audible.
4. **Logistics and Planning:** Careful planning is essential for a successful DX-pedition. This involves arranging transportation, accommodation, and power sources in remote locations, often far from urban centers.
5. **Patience and Perseverance:** DX-peditions can be challenging and frustrating, as conditions may not always align with expectations. Patience and perseverance are essential virtues for those who embark on these journeys.
6. **Community Collaboration:** Many DX-peditions involve collaboration with other enthusiasts. Working in teams can improve the chances of capturing rare signals and allows for shared expertise.

The Thrill of Rare DX

Rare DX, often used to describe the reception of stations from challenging or unusual locations, is the ultimate goal of DX-peditions and expeditions.

The allure of rare DX lies in the sense of accomplishment, the prestige within the shortwave radio community, and the treasure trove of verifications from stations that are seldom heard.

Here are some factors that make rare DX so appealing:

1. **Unpredictable Conditions:** Rare DX is elusive because it depends on a confluence of unpredictable factors, including atmospheric conditions, the time of day, and solar activity. This unpredictability makes capturing rare DX a true achievement.
2. **Validation of Skill:** Successfully receiving a rare station showcases the skill and expertise of the DXer. It demonstrates the ability to fine-tune equipment, exploit propagation, and master the nuances of shortwave listening.
3. **Coveted QSL Cards:** Rare DX stations often issue QSL cards that are highly sought after by collectors. These verifications serve as badges of honor, testaments to the DXer's dedication and perseverance.
4. **Global Recognition:** Achieving rare DX status brings global recognition within the shortwave radio community. DXers worldwide take note of these accomplishments and admire the dedication of those who capture rare signals.
5. **Satisfying the Curiosity:** DX-peditions often uncover hidden gems of programming, unique cultural insights, and local perspectives that might be otherwise inaccessible to the listener. These discoveries satiate the curiosity of the DXer.

Types of DX-Peditions and Expeditions

DX-peditions and expeditions are as diverse as the shortwave radio spectrum itself. While the primary objective is to capture rare signals, the approach and context can vary significantly. Here are some types of DX-peditions and expeditions:

1. **Remote Island DX-peditions:** Enthusiasts journey to remote islands or atolls, often situated far from urban areas and electromagnetic interference. These locations offer pristine conditions for shortwave listening.

2. **Mountain DX-peditions:** High-altitude expeditions take advantage of the unique propagation conditions found at elevated locations. These endeavors often require strenuous hikes and rigorous logistics.
3. **Desert DX-peditions:** Deserts offer wide, flat expanses that are conducive to long-distance signal propagation. DXers in deserts capitalize on the dry climate and minimal interference.
4. **Polar DX-peditions:** Expeditions to polar regions, such as the Arctic or Antarctic, present unique challenges and extraordinary opportunities for capturing signals from the far corners of the globe.
5. **Maritime DX-peditions:** Setting sail on the open seas, maritime expeditions involve traveling on ships to enhance shortwave listening conditions and access remote locations.
6. **Cultural Exploration Expeditions:** These expeditions prioritize cultural immersion, often involving visits to remote or unique communities. DXers aim to capture the cultural essence of these regions through radio programming.
7. **Archaeological Expeditions:** Some enthusiasts focus on locating and restoring historic radio equipment, such as vintage transmitters and antennas, in locations with rich radio history.

Notable DX-Peditions and Their Achievements

The history of DX-peditions is replete with remarkable achievements and records. These expeditions have brought forth rare DX that continues to captivate the shortwave radio community. Here are a few notable DX-peditions and their accomplishments:

1. **The Rockall DX-pedition:** In 1985, a DX-pedition set up on the uninhabited island of Rockall in the North Atlantic Ocean. This endeavor resulted in the capture of elusive signals from Asia, North America, and Oceania, earning the team worldwide acclaim.
2. **The Peter I Island DX-pedition:** Peter I Island, situated near Antarctica, was the destination of a DX-pedition in 1994. The

team received signals from 500 international broadcasters, covering 180 countries and territories.

3. **The Heard Island DX-pedition:** In 1997, a DX-pedition ventured to Heard Island in the Indian Ocean. The team successfully received over 700 shortwave broadcasts, including many rarely heard stations.

4. **The Bouvet Island DX-pedition:** Bouvet Island, one of the most remote and uninhabited places on Earth, has been the destination of multiple DX-peditions. These expeditions have captured numerous rare signals, making Bouvet a coveted destination for DXers.

5. **The Mount Athos DX-pedition:** Mount Athos, a monastic community in Greece, has been the site of several DX-peditions. These expeditions have uncovered a wealth of religious and cultural broadcasts unique to the region.

The Preparation and Planning

DX-peditions and expeditions require meticulous planning to maximize the chances of success. Here's an overview of the preparation involved:

1. **Location Scouting:** Choosing the right location is the foundation of a successful expedition. DXers often conduct extensive research, taking into account factors like radio interference, accessibility, and accommodation.

2. **Equipment Selection:** Specialized equipment is critical. This includes high-quality antennas, portable receivers, amplifiers, filters, and power sources capable of sustaining operations in remote areas.

3. **Logistics:** Coordinating transportation, accommodations, and supplies is essential. Many expeditions involve remote or challenging locations, necessitating careful logistics planning.

4. **Timing:** The timing of the expedition is influenced by propagation conditions. DXers monitor solar activity and atmospheric conditions to determine the most favorable periods for capturing rare signals.

5. **Community Collaboration:** Many DX-peditions involve collaboration with other enthusiasts. Teams work together to share knowledge, equipment, and responsibilities.
6. **Legal and Regulatory Compliance:** Understanding the legal and regulatory requirements of the destination country is crucial. Licensing, import restrictions, and customs regulations must be addressed.
7. **Safety and Health Considerations:** Safety should be a paramount concern. Expeditions to remote or extreme locations often require comprehensive safety measures, including emergency communication and medical provisions.

The Experience of a DX-Pedition

The actual experience of a DX-pedition is a culmination of careful planning, technical expertise, and the thrill of capturing rare DX. It's an adventure that takes the enthusiast far from the comforts of home, often into challenging environments.

Here's a glimpse into the experience of a DX-pedition:

1. **Setup and Antenna Deployment:** The first task upon arrival at the chosen location is to set up the equipment. This involves deploying antennas, establishing power sources, and configuring the receiver for optimal performance.
2. **Monitoring and Scanning:** DXers continuously monitor the airwaves, scanning the shortwave spectrum for signals of interest. They may employ various techniques, such as bandscanning, to capture signals from different frequency ranges.
3. **Signal Identification:** Identifying signals can be a complex task. DXers rely on their knowledge of station schedules, languages, music, and unique features to identify broadcasters.
4. **Signal Logging:** DXers maintain detailed logs of received signals, including frequency, date, time, and reception quality. These logs serve as valuable records of the expedition's achievements.

5. **QSL Requests:** Upon capturing rare signals, DXers often send reception reports to the broadcasting stations, seeking QSL cards as verification. This process involves detailed reporting of the received signal.
6. **Community Interaction:** Many DXers maintain communication with fellow enthusiasts during the expedition. They may share their experiences, signal logs, and reception reports with the community.
7. **Cultural and Natural Exploration:** DX-peditions often offer opportunities to explore the local culture and natural surroundings. Enthusiasts may immerse themselves in the local community or engage in nature activities during downtime.

The Rewards of DX-Peditions and Expeditions

The rewards of DX-peditions and expeditions extend far beyond the verification of rare DX. These adventures offer a myriad of personal and intellectual benefits:

1. **Sense of Achievement:** Successfully capturing rare signals brings a profound sense of accomplishment. DXers take pride in their ability to navigate the challenges and uncertainties of the ether.
2. **Cultural Enrichment:** DX-peditions often involve immersion in different cultures, languages, and communities. Enthusiasts gain a deeper appreciation of the global tapestry of human experiences.
3. **Skill Enhancement:** Engaging in DX-peditions hones shortwave listening skills. DXers become more adept at signal identification, propagation prediction, and equipment optimization.
4. **Community Recognition:** Accomplished DXers who share their findings and experiences with the community often earn recognition and respect from fellow enthusiasts.
5. **Memory and Camaraderie:** The memories of DX-peditions and expeditions, coupled with the bonds formed with fellow enthusiasts, endure long after the adventure is over.

6. **Cultural and Natural Exploration:** DX-peditions provide opportunities to explore and appreciate the unique cultural and natural features of the chosen location.
7. **Treasured QSL Cards:** Collecting QSL cards from rare DX captures forms a personal treasure trove that commemorates the achievements of the DXer.

A Passion That Endures

DX-peditions and expeditions are not endeavors for the faint of heart, but for those who embrace the challenges and uncertainties of these adventures, the rewards are immeasurable. The allure of rare DX, the camaraderie of fellow enthusiasts, and the opportunity to explore distant lands and cultures make DX-peditions a passion that endures for a lifetime.

As we navigate the ever-changing landscape of shortwave radio, one thing remains constant: the thrill of capturing elusive signals, the joy of QSL card verification, and the sense of wonder that draws enthusiasts to the ether in search of distant voices and hidden treasures. DX-peditions and expeditions are the pinnacle of this listener's journey, where the magic of radio waves converges with the thrill of discovery, making every expedition a memorable adventure in the world of shortwave radio mastery.

13.RECORDING AND ARCHIVING

Building Your Audio Library

S hortwave radio listening is a remarkable journey through the airwaves, connecting you to diverse cultures, languages, and music from around the world. The rich tapestry of broadcasts, news, music, and voices encountered during your listening sessions is a captivating experience. However, the ephemeral nature of radio means that many of these moments are fleeting, vanishing into the ether as soon as they're broadcast. This is where the practice of recording and archiving becomes essential for shortwave radio enthusiasts. In this article, we will explore the importance of building your audio library through recording and archiving, the tools and techniques involved, and the immense value of preserving the sonic snapshots of your listener's journey.

The Significance of Recording and Archiving

Recording and archiving your shortwave radio sessions is an invaluable practice with several significant benefits:

1. **Preserving History:** Shortwave broadcasts often capture historical events, local traditions, and cultural expressions. Archiving these recordings helps preserve a unique cultural and historical record.

2. **Revisiting Memories:** Recordings allow you to revisit your favorite broadcasts, catch up on missed content, or relive the experiences and emotions of memorable moments in your radio journey.

3. **Enhancing Learning:** Archiving broadcasts lets you analyze and study radio propagation, station schedules, language learning, and content analysis, deepening your understanding of the medium.
4. **Sharing with Others:** Archiving your recordings enables you to share interesting broadcasts, musical performances, or news segments with fellow enthusiasts or online communities.
5. **QSL Card Verification:** For those seeking QSL cards and verifications from stations, recordings provide concrete evidence of your reception, enhancing your chances of receiving these coveted verifications.
6. **Documenting Radio DX:** If you are engaged in DXing (the hobby of receiving distant or rare stations), archiving your logs and recordings is essential to maintain a historical record of your achievements.

Tools and Techniques for Recording

Building an audio library of shortwave radio recordings requires specific tools and techniques to capture the broadcasts effectively. Here's what you need to get started:

1. **Shortwave Radio Receiver:** A good-quality shortwave radio receiver is the heart of your recording setup. Ensure your radio has a line-out or headphone jack for connecting to your recording device.
2. **Recording Device:** You can use a variety of recording devices, including digital audio recorders, computers, or smartphones. Each has its advantages and limitations. Choose the one that suits your needs and budget.
3. **Cables and Connectors:** You'll need audio cables to connect your radio receiver to your recording device. Ensure you have the appropriate connectors for your setup, such as RCA or 3.5mm audio jacks.
4. **External Antenna:** To improve reception and reduce interference, consider using an external antenna. This can significantly enhance the quality of your recordings.

5. **Audio Editing Software:** Audio editing software is essential for cleaning up recordings, removing noise, enhancing audio quality, and segmenting recordings into individual files.
6. **Storage:** Archiving audio recordings can consume a significant amount of storage space. Invest in external hard drives or cloud storage solutions to ensure you have enough space for your library.

Recording Techniques

When recording shortwave radio broadcasts, consider the following techniques to improve the quality and accuracy of your recordings:

1. **Selecting the Right Frequency:** Choose the frequency and time of day carefully. Different stations and broadcasts are best received at specific frequencies and during particular propagation conditions.
2. **Avoiding Interference:** Minimize radio interference by selecting a quiet location for your setup. Reducing electromagnetic interference from household appliances and other electronics is crucial.
3. **Optimizing Antenna Placement:** Experiment with different antenna placements and orientations to find the best reception conditions. Outdoor antennas can significantly enhance your reception quality.
4. **Recording Format:** Choose an appropriate audio recording format, such as WAV or FLAC, to ensure high-quality recordings. Avoid lossy formats like MP3 if you want to preserve audio fidelity.
5. **Scheduled Recordings:** If you plan to capture specific broadcasts, schedule your recordings accordingly. This ensures you won't miss important programs or events.
6. **Noise Reduction:** After recording, use audio editing software to remove noise, hiss, and interference from your recordings. Noise reduction tools can enhance the clarity of your archived audio.

7. **Segmentation:** Segment your recordings into individual files for easy cataloging and retrieval. This is particularly important if you have a library of diverse content.

Organizing and Cataloging Your Audio Library

An efficiently organized audio library is essential for easy access and retrieval of your recorded shortwave radio content. Consider implementing the following strategies for cataloging your recordings:

1. **Naming Conventions:** Develop a consistent naming convention for your audio files. Include details like the date, time, frequency, and station name for easy identification.
2. **Folder Structure:** Create a well-structured folder hierarchy for your recordings. Organize content by date, frequency range, language, or station type, depending on your preferences.
3. **Metadata:** Embed metadata in your audio files, including details like the station name, broadcast title, language, and relevant notes. This information makes it easier to search for specific content.
4. **Database Software:** Consider using audio library management software or general database software to maintain a comprehensive catalog of your recordings. This can help you search and retrieve content efficiently.
5. **Backup:** Regularly back up your audio library to prevent data loss. Use external hard drives, cloud storage, or redundant storage solutions to ensure your recordings are protected.
6. **Documentation:** Maintain a log or journal alongside your audio library to document your listening experiences, reception conditions, and any relevant details about each recording.

Preserving Audio Quality

The quality of your shortwave radio recordings can significantly impact the value and usefulness of your archive. To preserve audio quality, follow these tips:

1. **Use High-Quality Equipment:** Invest in a high-quality shortwave radio receiver and a good recording device to capture clean, high-fidelity audio.
2. **External Antenna:** Use an external antenna to improve reception quality and minimize interference, resulting in clearer recordings.
3. **Lossless Formats:** Record in lossless audio formats like WAV or FLAC to retain the highest audio quality. Avoid using compressed formats like MP3, which can degrade audio fidelity.
4. **Noise Reduction:** After recording, apply noise reduction and audio cleanup using editing software to enhance the audio quality.
5. **Bit Depth and Sample Rate:** Capture audio at higher bit depths and sample rates, such as 24-bit and 96kHz, to preserve as much detail as possible.
6. **Storage:** Use high-capacity and reliable storage solutions to avoid compression or quality loss due to insufficient space.
7. **Preservation Format:** Consider creating preservation copies of your most valuable recordings in a lossless format and keep them in a separate archive to ensure long-term audio fidelity.

Sharing and Collaborating

Sharing your shortwave radio recordings with others and collaborating with fellow enthusiasts can enhance your listening journey and contribute to the broader shortwave radio community. Here's how to do it effectively:

1. **Online Forums and Communities:** Participate in online forums and communities dedicated to shortwave radio. These platforms provide a space to share recordings, discuss content, and collaborate with other enthusiasts.
2. **Social Media:** Share snippets or highlights from your recordings on social media platforms to engage with a broader audience and connect with like-minded individuals.
3. **Collaborative Projects:** Collaborate with other enthusiasts on specific recording projects, such as capturing rare stations,

unique broadcasts, or cultural events. Joint efforts can yield exceptional results.

4. **Recording Exchange:** Share and exchange recordings with other enthusiasts to expand your audio library and discover content you might have missed.

5. **Contributing to Online Archives:** Contribute your recordings to online shortwave radio archives, where they can be accessed and enjoyed by a global audience.

6. **Broadcast Monitoring Networks:** Participate in international broadcast monitoring networks to report on station schedules, signal quality, and programming content. Your contributions can benefit the entire community.

Legality and Ethical Considerations

When recording and archiving shortwave radio broadcasts, it's crucial to be aware of the legal and ethical considerations surrounding this practice:

1. **Copyright:** Be mindful of copyright laws and regulations when recording and sharing content. Some broadcasts may be protected by copyright, and unauthorized distribution could be illegal.

2. **Non-Commercial Use:** In many cases, personal, non-commercial use of recorded broadcasts is acceptable. However, it's essential to check and understand the copyright and usage policies of the station or broadcaster.

3. **Verification:** If you intend to seek QSL card verifications, it's important to follow the broadcaster's verification procedures and submit accurate reception reports along with your recording.

4. **Ethical Use:** Always respect the privacy and rights of individuals and organizations whose content you record. Ensure that your recordings are used in an ethical and responsible manner.

5. **Attribution:** When sharing or distributing recordings, give proper attribution to the station or broadcaster, and provide any relevant information or metadata.

Conclusion

Recording and archiving your shortwave radio listening sessions is a rewarding and enriching practice that deepens your engagement with the medium. It allows you to capture and preserve unique cultural expressions, historical events, and captivating broadcasts that might otherwise be lost in the ether.

By investing in high-quality equipment, employing effective recording techniques, and maintaining a well-organized library, you can build a valuable archive of shortwave radio content. Sharing your recordings and collaborating with fellow enthusiasts enhances your listening journey and contributes to the broader shortwave radio community.

As you continue your listener's journey through the airwaves, remember that each recording is a sonic snapshot of a moment in time, a testament to the magic of radio waves, and a testament to the rich diversity of voices and stories that fill the shortwave ether. Your audio library is a treasure trove of these moments, and it will continue to grow and evolve as you explore the boundless world of shortwave radio mastery.

14.RADIO AS A HOBBY

Collecting and Restoring Vintage Receivers

Shortwave radio listening is a fascinating and immersive hobby that connects enthusiasts to a world of diverse cultures, news, music, and stories from around the globe. While modern shortwave radios provide excellent performance and convenience, there's a unique charm in collecting and restoring vintage receivers. These iconic pieces of radio history not only allow you to tune in to distant broadcasts but also serve as windows to the past, preserving the legacy of radio technology and design. In this article, we will delve into the captivating world of collecting and restoring vintage receivers, exploring the allure of these timeless machines, the process of finding and refurbishing them, and the joy of reliving the golden age of radio.

The Allure of Vintage Receivers

Vintage shortwave receivers hold an irresistible appeal for radio enthusiasts. There are several reasons behind the enduring fascination with these classic machines:

1. **Historical Significance:** Vintage radios are tangible pieces of history, representing the evolution of radio technology. Each receiver tells a story of the era in which it was manufactured, the design trends of the time, and the role of radio in society.
2. **Craftsmanship:** Many vintage receivers are renowned for their exceptional craftsmanship and attention to detail. These

machines were often hand-built with high-quality materials, resulting in robust and durable construction.

3. **Aesthetic Beauty:** Vintage radios often feature iconic designs and elegant cabinet work. They are not just functional devices but also decorative pieces that add character and charm to any room.

4. **Audio Quality:** The vacuum tube technology used in vintage radios can produce a warm, rich sound that many enthusiasts find more appealing than the audio from modern solid-state radios.

5. **Simplicity:** Vintage receivers are renowned for their simplicity and ease of use. Many are devoid of the complex digital interfaces found in modern radios, allowing listeners to focus on the core experience of tuning in to broadcasts.

6. **Nostalgia:** For some, vintage radios evoke feelings of nostalgia, harkening back to a time when radio was the primary source of news, entertainment, and companionship in the home.

7. **Technical Challenge:** Collecting and restoring vintage radios can be a technical and rewarding hobby. It involves problem-solving, electronics knowledge, and hands-on skills.

The Journey of Collecting Vintage Receivers

The journey of collecting vintage receivers begins with a passion for radio history and a love for the art of preservation. Here are the essential steps to get started:

1. **Research and Education:** Begin by learning about the history of radio technology, the key milestones in receiver design, and the notable manufacturers of vintage radios. Books, online resources, and radio history enthusiasts are valuable sources of information.

2. **Define Your Interests:** Decide on the era, style, and specific receivers that interest you the most. Whether you prefer the art deco designs of the 1930s or the mid-century modern aesthetics of the 1950s, narrowing down your focus will make collecting more manageable.

3. **Join Radio Enthusiast Communities:** Connecting with other radio enthusiasts is invaluable. Online forums, local clubs, and social media groups provide opportunities to share knowledge, exchange advice, and discover sources for vintage radios.
4. **Scouting and Sourcing:** Vintage radios can be found in various places, including estate sales, garage sales, antique shops, online auctions, and dedicated radio fairs. Scouring these sources can lead to unexpected finds.
5. **Evaluation and Inspection:** When considering a vintage radio, inspect it thoroughly. Check for any visible damage, missing parts, or signs of wear and tear. If possible, power on the radio to assess its functionality.
6. **Assessment of Restoration Needs:** Vintage radios often require restoration work due to their age. Assess the extent of restoration needed, such as replacing capacitors, cleaning the chassis, or refinishing the cabinet.
7. **Negotiation and Acquisition:** Negotiate the price with the seller and acquire the radio that best fits your collection and restoration goals. Some radios may be in pristine condition, while others are sold as restoration projects.

The Art of Restoration

Restoring vintage radios is an art that requires patience, technical skills, and a keen appreciation for preserving history. The restoration process typically includes the following steps:

1. **Dismantling:** Begin by carefully disassembling the radio. Document the placement of components and take photographs to aid in reassembly.
2. **Cleaning:** Thoroughly clean the chassis, cabinet, and all components. Remove dust, grime, and any corrosion on metal parts.
3. **Electronic Repairs:** Vintage radios often have components that need replacement or repair. Common issues include malfunctioning capacitors, resistors, and vacuum tubes. Replace faulty components to ensure proper functionality.

4. **Resistor and Capacitor Replacement:** Over time, resistors and capacitors may have drifted in value. Replacing these components with modern equivalents can improve the radio's performance.
5. **Tube Testing:** Vacuum tubes are critical components of vintage radios. Test each tube to ensure it's operating within the specified parameters. Replace tubes that are faulty or weak.
6. **Alignment and Calibration:** Vintage radios require proper alignment and calibration to ensure they receive signals accurately. Use specialized equipment, such as an oscilloscope and signal generator, to adjust the radio's circuits.
7. **Cosmetic Restoration:** If the cabinet or dial face is damaged, consider refinishing or repainting them to restore their original appearance. This can greatly enhance the visual appeal of the radio.
8. **Final Inspection:** After completing the restoration work, perform a final inspection of the radio. Ensure all components are in their correct positions, and check for any loose connections or wiring issues.
9. **Powering On:** Gradually power on the radio while monitoring for any signs of trouble, such as smoke, unusual sounds, or sparking. If everything appears normal, let the radio warm up and test its reception capabilities.
10. **Cabinet Reassembly:** Reassemble the cabinet and ensure it is securely fastened. Clean the glass or plastic dial cover, knobs, and any other external components.
11. **Documentation:** Keep detailed records of the restoration process, including the replacement of components, adjustments made, and any challenges encountered.
12. **Enjoyment and Display:** Once the restoration is complete, enjoy your vintage radio by tuning in to shortwave broadcasts and relishing the aesthetic beauty of these iconic machines.

Challenges and Considerations

While restoring vintage radios can be a deeply rewarding hobby, it comes with its set of challenges and considerations:

1. **Availability of Parts:** Some components, especially vacuum tubes, may be challenging to find, and certain models may require specialized parts that are no longer in production.
2. **Technical Expertise:** A sound understanding of electronics and radio technology is crucial for successful restoration. If you lack experience, consider seeking guidance from experienced enthusiasts or professional restorers.
3. **Safety Precautions:** Working with vintage radios involves electrical components and voltages that can pose safety risks. Always take proper precautions and ensure that you are familiar with safe restoration practices.
4. **Budget:** Restoration can be costly, particularly if the radio requires extensive repairs or the replacement of rare components. Budget considerations are essential.
5. **Originality vs. Functionality:** Deciding whether to prioritize the originality of a vintage radio or its functionality is a common dilemma. Some collectors prefer radios in pristine, untouched condition, while others focus on ensuring they work flawlessly.
6. **Storage and Display:** Vintage radios can be delicate, and their cabinets are susceptible to damage. Ensure you have a safe and dust-free environment for storing and displaying your collection.

Preserving the Legacy of Vintage Radios

Collecting and restoring vintage receivers is not just a personal hobby; it is a vital contribution to the preservation of radio history. Vintage radios are cultural artifacts that represent an era when radio was the primary source of news, entertainment, and communication. By keeping these radios in working condition, enthusiasts ensure that future generations can appreciate the history and technological innovation that defined radio's golden age.

Moreover, vintage radios continue to serve as functional shortwave receivers. By restoring and using them, enthusiasts keep the tradition of shortwave radio listening alive, tuning in to broadcasts from around the world and enjoying the warm, nostalgic sound of these classic machines.

Conclusion

Collecting and restoring vintage receivers is a passion that blends history, craftsmanship, and technical expertise. Each vintage radio is a window into the past, offering insights into the era in which it was created and the role of radio in society. The art of restoration allows enthusiasts to preserve these iconic machines, ensuring that they continue to tell their stories for generations to come.

As you embark on your journey of collecting and restoring vintage receivers, you become a guardian of radio history, a curator of craftsmanship, and a connoisseur of shortwave listening. With every successful restoration, you not only bring a piece of the past back to life but also create new memories and experiences in the present. Your vintage receivers are more than just radio sets; they are time machines that transport you to the golden age of radio, where the airwaves were filled with the voices of the world, waiting to be heard and cherished.

15. THE FUTURE OF SHORTWAVE

Trends and Challenges

Shortwave radio has long been a fascinating medium that connects listeners to voices and cultures from around the world. For decades, enthusiasts have explored the magic of shortwave radio, but the landscape is evolving. As technology and communication methods advance, the future of shortwave radio faces both promising trends and significant challenges. In this article, we will delve into the potential future of shortwave radio, examining emerging trends, the impact of digital technology, and the unique challenges that enthusiasts, broadcasters, and the medium itself must confront in the coming years.

Trends in Shortwave Radio

While shortwave radio faces challenges, several trends are shaping its future, offering opportunities for enthusiasts and broadcasters to adapt and thrive. Let's explore some of these trends:

1. **Digital Modes and Data Transmission:** The integration of digital modes has breathed new life into shortwave radio. Data modes like FT8 and DRM (Digital Radio Mondiale) allow for more efficient and reliable transmission of text, images, and even multimedia content over shortwave frequencies. This trend enhances the practicality and versatility of shortwave radio, making it relevant for data transmission alongside traditional voice broadcasts.

2. **Emergency Communications:** Shortwave radio remains a vital tool for emergency communication in regions with limited infrastructure. As natural disasters and humanitarian crises become more frequent, shortwave radio's role in providing information and enabling communication during such events is likely to grow.

3. **DXing and Expeditionary Listening:** The pursuit of distant or rare stations, known as DXing, continues to be a vibrant aspect of shortwave radio. DX-peditions and expeditions, where enthusiasts travel to remote locations to capture elusive signals, also contribute to the appeal of the hobby. The camaraderie and sense of adventure in these endeavours are trends that add excitement to shortwave listening.

4. **Cultural Discovery and Niche Content:** Shortwave radio is celebrated for its ability to provide access to unique, niche content. As some broadcasters move online or cease shortwave transmissions, others recognize the enduring value of reaching global audiences through shortwave. Cultural and niche programming will likely continue to thrive, offering listeners a diverse array of content.

5. **Community Building:** Online forums, social media groups, and enthusiast communities have allowed listeners to connect, share experiences, and support one another. The sense of belonging to a global community of shortwave radio enthusiasts is a trend that fosters enthusiasm for the medium.

Challenges Facing Shortwave Radio

Despite these promising trends, shortwave radio also confronts various challenges that impact its future:

1. **Digital Migration:** As digital technology becomes more pervasive; some broadcasters are opting to transition from shortwave to digital platforms. While digital modes offer advantages, the transition can mean the loss of traditional shortwave broadcasts.

2. **Interference and Spectrum Crowding:** Shortwave radio bands are susceptible to interference from various sources, including industrial and electrical equipment, unintentional radiators, and even deliberate jamming by governments. Spectrum crowding poses challenges for broadcasters and listeners alike.

3. **Aging Infrastructure:** Many shortwave broadcasting facilities and transmission sites are aging and require substantial maintenance and investment. Some countries have chosen to decommission or reduce their shortwave transmissions due to these infrastructure challenges.

4. **Declining Listener Base:** The accessibility and convenience of digital media, such as streaming services and podcasts, have led to a decline in the number of shortwave listeners. Younger generations may not be as familiar with or drawn to the medium.

5. **Content Fragmentation:** The shift toward digital modes and data transmission has led to a fragmentation of content. While this allows for niche programming, it can also result in less accessibility to general news and information on shortwave.

6. **Regulatory Challenges:** Shortwave broadcasters must navigate international regulations and coordination to ensure that they do not interfere with other broadcasts. These regulatory challenges can be complex and time-consuming.

Adapting to the Future

To ensure the continued relevance and vitality of shortwave radio, enthusiasts, broadcasters, and organizations must adapt to the changing landscape. Here are several ways in which the future of shortwave radio can be positively shaped:

1. **Embrace Digital Modes:** Embracing digital modes and data transmission can enhance shortwave radio's utility. Enthusiasts and broadcasters should explore the potential of data modes like DRM and the broader digital radio landscape.

2. **Promote Emergency Communication:** Highlighting shortwave radio's role in emergency communication and preparedness can increase its importance and value, especially in regions prone to natural disasters and political instability.
3. **Attract a New Generation:** To attract a younger audience, shortwave radio enthusiasts and organizations can develop educational programs, online resources, and events that showcase the unique appeal of the medium.
4. **Advocate for the Spectrum:** Enthusiasts and organizations should advocate for the preservation of shortwave radio spectrum and work to mitigate interference and jamming issues.
5. **Preserve Radio History:** Efforts to document and preserve the history of shortwave radio, including the stories of legendary broadcasters and iconic receivers, can help ensure that the medium's legacy endures.
6. **Invest in Infrastructure:** Broadcasters should invest in maintaining and upgrading their transmission facilities, making shortwave broadcasts more reliable and accessible.
7. **Collaboration and Innovation:** Collaboration among shortwave broadcasters, enthusiasts, and organizations can foster innovation and the development of new technologies, ensuring the medium's ongoing relevance.
8. **Education and Awareness:** Initiatives to raise awareness about shortwave radio's unique qualities and benefits can contribute to its sustained popularity.

The Future of Shortwave Radio: A Blend of Tradition and Technology

The future of shortwave radio is a dynamic blend of tradition and technology. While some challenges loom, the enduring appeal of shortwave radio—connecting listeners across vast distances, providing access to cultural diversity, and serving as a vital tool in emergencies—will continue to shape its place in the modern world. The convergence of traditional broadcasting with digital modes and data transmission offers exciting possibilities for shortwave radio's future.

As shortwave radio enthusiasts, we have a responsibility to safeguard and advance the legacy of this unique medium. The future of shortwave radio is not just the responsibility of broadcasters or regulatory bodies; it is also in the hands of the global community of shortwave listeners who share a passion for this enduring and captivating form of communication.

In the end, the future of shortwave radio is a story that continues to unfold, and it is a story that we, as listeners and enthusiasts, have the power to influence and shape. Whether you're tuning in to a broadcast from a remote corner of the globe, capturing elusive DX, or sharing your experiences with a global community of fellow enthusiasts, you are a part of this evolving narrative. Together, we can ensure that the magic of shortwave radio remains vibrant and resonant, continuing to connect us to the world and its ever-changing stories.

Milton Keynes UK
Ingram Content Group UK Ltd.
UKHW050637161123
432684UK00014B/466